Educating for
Cultural Competence

Educating for Cultural Competence
TOOLS FOR TRAINING FIELD INSTRUCTORS

Marilyn Peterson Armour

Bonnie Bain

Ruth J. Rubio

Council on Social Work Education
Alexandria, Virginia

Copyright © 2006, Council on Social Work Education, Inc.

Published in the United States by the Council on Social Work Education, Inc. All rights reserved. No part of this book may be reproduced or transmitted in any manner whatsoever without the prior written permission of the publisher.

Library of Congress Cataloguing-in-Publication Data

Armour, Marilyn Peterson.
  Educating for cultural competence : tools for training field instructors / Marilyn Peterson Armour, Bonnie Bain, Ruth Rubio.
     p. cm.
  Includes bibliographical references and index.
  ISBN 0-87293-122-6
  1. Social work education. 2. Social service–Field work. 3. Social work with minorities–Study and teaching (Internship) 4. Social workers–Supervision of. I. Bain, Bonnie. II. Rubio, Ruth. III. Council on Social Work Education. IV. Title.
  HV11.A68 2006
  361.3071'55–dc22
                                    2006010442

ISBN 0-87293-122-6

Printed in the United States of America on acid-free paper that meets the American National Standards Institute Z39-48 Standard.

Council on Social Work Education, Inc.
1725 Duke Street, Suite 500
Alexandria, VA 22314-3457
www.cswe.org

Contents

Preface **vii**

PART 1 GETTING STARTED **1**

Introduction **1**

Chapter 1 Cornerstone Concepts **3**

Chapter 2 Overview of Training **7**

Chapter 3 Training Team Meetings **11**

Chapter 4 Planning and Preparation **13**

Chapter 5 Implementation **19**

PART 2 RELATIONSHIP WITH SELF **23**

Chapter 6 Module 1: Welcoming Diversity in Self **24**

Chapter 7 Module 2: Taking a Stand for Diversity **36**

PART 3 RELATIONSHIP WITH STUDENT SUPERVISEE **45**

Chapter 8 Module 3: Exploring Diversity in the Supervisory Relationship **47**

Chapter 9 Module 4: Effecting Change in the Supervisory Relationship **56**

PART 4 RELATIONSHIP WITH AGENCY **67**

Chapter 10 Module 5: Diversity and Your Agency **69**

Chapter 11 Module 6: Future Action **76**

PART 5 WRAP-UP **85**

Chapter 12 Closing Statement **86**

References **88**

Appendix A Seven Formats: Full and Modified Designs With Consecutive and Intermittent Schedules **93**

Appendix B Handout: Being Direct in Supervision **108**
Appendix C Supervision Role-Playing Examples **111**
Appendix D Worksheet: Assessing the Cultural Competence of the Agency **113**
Appendix E Ending and Follow-Up **114**
Appendix F Agency Competence **115**
Appendix G Recommended Articles **118**
Appendix H Handout: Racial Identity Development **120**
Appendix I Summary of NASW Standards for Cultural Competence in Social Work Practice **122**
Appendix J Recommended Reading **124**

Preface

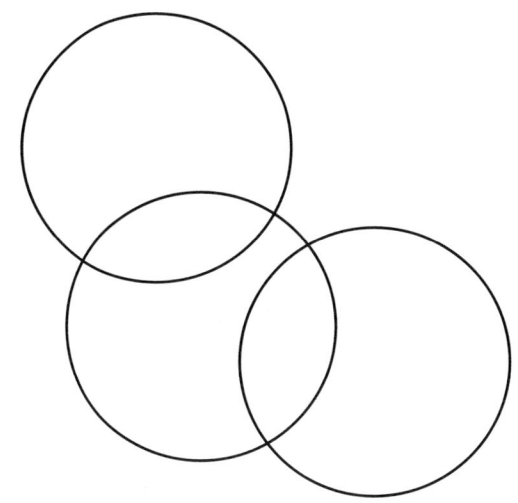

Since 1968, the Council on Social Work Education (CSWE) has required schools of social work to achieve cultural diversity in enrollment of students, hiring of faculty, and development of curricula (McMahon & Allen-Meares, 1992). The National Association of Social Workers has published standards in cultural competence that oblige social workers to strive to deliver culturally competent services to increasingly diverse client populations (NASW, 2001). Through its curriculum policy statement, CSWE provides a broad mandate for the infusion of multicultural content into academic courses (Carrillo, Holzhalb, & Thyer, 1993; Julia, 2000). It is, however, in the application of knowledge about cultural and social differences through a supervised internship or work environment that the training in multicultural competencies is integrated (Van Soest, 2004).

Under the 2002 CSWE *Education Policy and Accreditation Standards* (EPAS), students are expected to demonstrate mastery of culturally competent practice concepts (Fong & Lum, 2004). According to Lum (2003), these concepts include cultural awareness, knowledge acquisition, skill development, and continuous inductive learning within the context of strengths extracted from each culture's value system (Fong & Furuto, 2001). More recently, scholars have challenged social work educators to include social justice concepts as well, for example, privilege, racism, and oppression (Priddy, 2004; Van Soest, 2004). At the time of placement, accordingly, students should be primed and ready to use these concepts in their practicum sites.

Although it is well recognized that field is the curricular area most suited to incorporating cultural content into the student's practice (Manoleas, 2004; Van Soest, 2004), field instructors may not be comfortable with their own multicultural competence and may not purposefully engage students about these pertinent issues or consider them to be important (Marshack, Hendricks, & Gladstein, 1994;

Priddy, 2004). Field instructors who do not feel adequate may reduce their anxieties by avoiding such issues (Manoleas, 2004). Possible discussions between students and field instructors may dead-end, and students may miss valuable opportunities for growth if field instructors avoid or are acutely self-conscious when addressing cross-cultural issues, including differences between them and their students (Hendricks, 2003). Students may replicate these responses by ignoring or minimizing important differences between themselves and their clients, covering up their ineptness, or responding mechanically.

In spite of the fact that the role of field instructor is considered pivotal to how students learn to address issues of diversity and oppression (Dean & Fleck-Henderson, 1992; Dore, 1993; Freeman & Valentine, 1998; Raske, 1999), little practical information exists to guide field instructors on how to integrate multiculturalism into the supervision process (Arkin, 1999; Cashwell, Looby, & Housley, 1997; Leong & Wagner, 1994). Indeed, only a small number of articles have addressed the issues relevant to supervising for culturally competent practice (e.g., Gladstein & Mailick, 1986; Hendricks, 2003; Marshack, Hendricks, & Gladstein, 1994; McRoy, Freeman, Logan, & Blackmon, 1986; Ryan & Hendricks, 1989; Solomon, 1982).

This training manual begins to fill that gap. It was written expressly for field instructors. The particular approach used in the training was developed in response to an annual end-of-year survey of field instructors ($n=52$) that showed disparities in the ability of both students and field instructors to discuss cultural issues *directly* with each other despite the students' familiarity with classroom content on cultural and social diversity and field instructors' and students' exposure to clients and staff who were different from them (Bain & Garcia, 1999). This finding indicates that the priority in training needs to be on understanding and addressing factors that might promote staying away from a potentially volatile topic. These factors are referred to as "avoidant behaviors." Instead of being a deliberate act of evasion or indicator of psychopathology, avoidance is seen as a natural reaction to situations that create discomfort, self-doubt, and the potential for judgment and criticism of a person's attitudes and behaviors. The purpose of this manual, therefore, is to provide field instructors with tools to intervene on their natural avoidance of the discomfort that accompanies working on cultural and social diversity issues with students. In turn, field instructors will be better equipped to help students get outside their comfort zone in order to meaningfully address differences with clients, recognize and intervene on oppressive practices and behaviors, and promote social justice.

The training is divided into three themes that reflect the real world in which field instructors work and teach:

1. Relationship With Self
2. Relationship With Student Supervisee
3. Relationship With Agency

The training addresses manifestations of avoidance of cultural and social diversity in each of the themes with the goal of enabling field instructors to be more effective teachers. The training is experiential and skill based. It uses mini lectures, graduated exercises, and discussions to teach skills specific to the supervisory relationship and to deconstruct and rework cognitions that otherwise hinder direct and proactive responses to social and cultural diversity. This approach is supported by the literature that emphasizes the use of active learning for infusing cultural diversity into field instruction (e.g., Armour, Bain, & Rubio, 2004; Helms & Cook, 1999; Kim & Leong, 1991; McChesney & Euster, 2000; Porter, 1994; Walters, Strom-Gottfried, & Sullivan, 1998).

The training consists of six modules that are delivered in a variety of flexible time formats to accommodate each school's needs. Although schools may experiment with the content and formats, the training is specialized, intentionally sequential, and was not developed for partial inclusion in other training, such as the introductory training for field instructors offered by many schools of social work. The training is time intensive because it targets entrenched and culturally sanctioned behavior and requires the introduction and repetition of new constructs and the creation of a validating community for change to occur. The time commitment necessary for this training is supported by Miller, Hyde, and Ruth (2004), who state, "Multicultural classes that do not provide time for introspection, empathy and other emotional tasks are providing students with only intellectual tools and learning will remain shallow" (p. 419).

This training has been implemented with three different groups: (1) an ethnically diverse group, (2) a homogeneous group that was predominantly White, and (3) a homogeneous group that was predominantly African American. A 13-item survey was developed and administered three times (pretraining, posttraining, and six-month follow-up) to field instructors in the predominantly White group. It addressed three dimensions of decreased avoidance: comfort with diversity, attention to issues of power and control and interpersonal conflict, and knowledge about "oppressed" groups. Evaluation of the training showed significant decreases in avoidant behavior over time (Wilks$^\wedge$=.45, $F(2,9)=5.4$, $p=.02$) (Armour, Bain, &

Rubio, 2004). Field directors from 10 schools of social work have reviewed the manual. Their feedback has been incorporated into the training design.

CSWE has long recognized the need for culturally competent practice. In 1999, Lum introduced a self-assessment instrument to measure competencies. Several authors have made major textbook contributions that are widely used in the field (e.g., Fong, 2004; Fong & Furuto, 2001; Gutiérrez, Zuñiga, & Lum, 2004; Lum, 2003, 2005). A number of academicians have addressed teaching social justice and diversity content in the classroom (e.g., Holley & Steiner, 2005; Hyde & Ruth, 2002; Miller et al., 2004; Mishna & Rasmussen, 2001; Van Soest, 2004; Van Soest & Garcia, 2003). Although there has been recognition that the field practicum is critical to the development of multicultural competencies and provides unique opportunities for students to integrate theory and practice (Van Soest, 2004), the cultural competence of field instructors has been assumed. Moreover, because few if any schools offer specialized training, field instructors have been left to fend for themselves without the educational support to address those issues related to cultural and social differences and the power and privilege that can occur with particular intensity in the field instructor-student relationship. The investment of time in this specialized training for field instructors can have a major return if their students are the recipients and are better equipped to help the increasingly diverse client populations that they, as social workers, will serve.

PART 1

Getting Started

Introduction

Welcome to the Collaborative Training Model for developing cultural competence in social work field education. The collaborative model promotes effective teaching and enables field instructors to integrate knowledge about cultural competence into the social work student's field experience. In today's world, cultural competence in field education is essential to prepare students for effective social work practice with ever-increasing diverse populations that are different from the students.

The cornerstone concepts for this model are as follows:

- Collaboration between the university and the practice community
- Collaboration between trainers and field instructors
- Articulation and acceptance of the relationship between anxiety and the avoidance inherent in the process of becoming more culturally competent
- Importance of celebrating ourselves as a necessary first step toward celebrating differences
- Skill development to increase comfort and ability to deal directly with sensitive differences
- A deliberate, open-ended planning process

The model is organized around three themes as the context for social work practice and training: Relationship With Self, Relationship With Student Supervisee, and Relationship With Agency. Culture—as it is used in this model—is broadly defined to include ethnicity, race, national origin, social class, age, sexual orientation, gender identity, religion, family structure, and mental or physical disability (NASW, 2001). This model encourages expanded awareness of the concept of cultural and social diversity to include "hidden" differences, such as use of language, immigration status, and skin color variation. Other less than obvious differences could include mental disabilities, birth order, and sexual orientation and gender identity. The model also recognizes the concept of multiple identities and the systemic dynamics of oppression based on other identities such as gender, ethnicity, class, sexual orientation, ability, and religion (Van Soest, 2004). As Van Soest notes,

> Cultural competence refers to the process by which individuals and systems respond respectfully and effectively to people of all cultures, languages, classes, races, ethnic backgrounds, religions, and other diversity factors in a manner that recognizes, affirms, and values the worth of individuals, families, and communities and protects and preserves the dignity of each. (NASW, 2001)

In this training, the development of diversity and cultural competence skills are used interchangeably.

Throughout the manual, field instructors are referred to as "participants."

The authors would like to acknowledge the following schools of social work for their contribution to the refinement of this model: Baylor School of Social Work, California State University-Fresno, Columbia University, University of California at Berkeley, Florida International University, Kean University, University of Minnesota, Texas A&M International University, University of Vermont, and the University of Wyoming. The authors are particularly indebted to the George Warren Brown School of Social Work at Washington University in St. Louis, and the University of Missouri-St. Louis for their collaboration with us in applying the model and providing comprehensive feedback. Finally, the authors express their appreciation to Deanna Cox, Polly Brown, and Patricia Dolan for their assistance.

CHAPTER 1

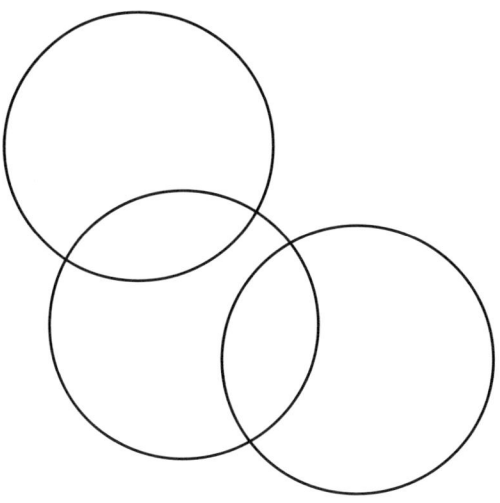

Cornerstone Concepts

Collaboration Between the University and the Practice Community

The Collaborative Training Model rests on a partnership between the university and the practice community that develops over the duration of the training. Specifically, university trainers inquire into and respond to the needs of participants from the practice community, so that field instructors from the practice community can immediately apply what they learn to field education. Trainers must show, therefore, that they are genuinely interested in learning from field instructors about their professional struggles, opportunities, and obstacles in teaching cultural competence in their settings. The teaching/learning experience is introduced as intentionally interactional and collaborative as the name of the model implies. This open partnership maximizes the possibility for mutual trust, growth, and change in both trainer and trainee.

Collaboration Between Trainers and Participants

It is important to minimize perceptions of hierarchy between trainers and participants in order to establish a sense of collaboration and safety for risking honest reflection and sharing. Toward that end, trainers are to equalize the relationship by emphasizing that *all* social workers have an ethical commitment to engage continually in the process of becoming more culturally competent (NASW, 1999). Trainer self-disclosure throughout the training experience is an effective way to demonstrate that this process is never ending; for example, there are no graduates in cultural competence if social workers live according to social work values. From the beginning, the message to the field instructors is: "We are all in this together. We are all works in progress."

Normalizing Anxiety and Avoidance

No one can sincerely engage in the struggle to become more culturally competent without experiencing some anxiety in the process. Common triggers include the following:

- Fear of being unintentionally offending in attempting to identify or discuss diversity issues
- Feelings of guilt
- Painful experiences
- Fear of exposing one's hidden biases
- Dissonance between beliefs and actions

The normalization of anxiety and the human tendency to avoid what is uncomfortable or anxiety producing is a central organizing theme throughout the training. It is predicated on the belief that naming sensitive issues that are usually avoided—the elephant in the room—enables participants to accept and push through their anxiety rather than shut down or withdraw from the process when it becomes uncomfortable. Trainers are encouraged to bring a statue of an elephant to each session and place it in plain sight, so that everyone has a visual reminder of the human tendency to avoid what is uncomfortable. Moreover, participants' ability and willingness to discuss candidly the anxiety involved in their diversity work is encouraged by reframing their acknowledgment as an indication of their sincerity and motivation to grow in becoming culturally competent.

Celebrating Differences

In American mainstream culture, the values of rugged individualism and competition, the domination of dualistic thinking, and ethnocentrism are inescapable influences in shaping attitudes and approaches to diversity. Moreover, since we are taught to think of diversity as creating problems, we tend to react in ways that ignore or minimize the differences among us. This point is illustrated by such statements as the following:

- "I don't have any culture. I am just American."
- "We are all human, so why don't we emphasize how we are all alike instead of talking about how we are different?"

Celebrating differences includes the sometimes painful process of becoming aware of the many ways all of us are affected by unearned privilege and oppression in this society (Gutiérrez & Nagda, 1996; Hyde & Ruth, 2002; Lum, 1999; Miller et al., 2004; Van Soest, 2004). Indeed, because we all have multiple social identities, people are both targets of oppression and agents of oppression (Bell, 1997). For this training model, privilege is defined as unearned entitlements for a certain group and exclusion of others, such as limited employment opportunities for older people. Privilege also includes conferred dominance, which gives one group power over another, such as people who are able in contrast to people with disabilities (McIntosh, 1993).

This model incorporates the idea that people are better able to welcome and celebrate differences if these differences are positively reinforced, and people are encouraged to recognize that they take pride in the characteristics that define their own cultural groups and heritage (Pinderhughes, 1989). The Collaborative Training Model starts by establishing, therefore, a safe place for participants to risk themselves in reflection and dialogue with each other and to make overt the internalization of beliefs that result in being alienated or ashamed of one's own culture.

Skill Development for Directly Dealing With Differences

A survey of field instructors and their students found that both groups had difficulty directly addressing diversity issues in supervision despite exposure to ethnically diverse client populations (Bain & Garcia, 1999). The Collaborative Training Model uses the concept of parallel process with participants to model what they must do with students. Specifically, participants must push through their anxiety to demonstrate how to deal directly with issues of diversity in their supervisory relationships with social work students (Torres & Jones, 1997). Students then can mirror the process with clients by drawing on the internalized experience they have had in supervision (Doehrman, 1976). It is not enough, therefore, for trainers merely to articulate the idea of the need to be open and direct with students in raising issues related to diversity. Rather, agency field instructors must acquire specific skills for actively engaging their students in examining cultural differences. It is through the acquisition of these skills that field instructors' anxiety levels are decreased and confidence is raised. The more skillful and confident the field instructor feels in identifying and discussing cultural and social diversity issues, the more likely he or she is to deal with these issues directly with students. By *directly*, we mean the ability to be appropriately open and candid about differences. We also recognize that some cultures do not value directness. We therefore recommend that field instructors be aware of the mores within their own cultural context and derive strategies for addressing a student's learning needs that include sensitivity to a variety of communication styles.

The Open-Ended Planning Process

Although the training follows a semistructured agenda, sessions are planned based on behavioral observations of participants and their responses to the material presented. Specifically, the training addresses manifestations of participants' anxiety and avoidance in three areas: Relationship With Self, Relationship With Student Supervisee, and Relationship With Agency. Since the manifestation of avoidance is highly individualized and varies by participant and subject matter, an open-ended planning process is used to tailor the training to the needs of the participants, their experiences, and the level of their comfort or discomfort with the issues. This strategy both engages participants at a personal level and allows material to be more relevant and meaningful. Key questions for trainers at the end of every session include:

- Where was participation most enthusiastic?
- Where did there seem to be the most resistance?
- What is known about the various participants' levels of cultural competence?
- Where is the group as a whole?
- What do we need to do to help participants acknowledge and push through their anxiety?

Answers to these questions provide the basis for planning upcoming sessions and ensuring individualized responses to the participants. Uniqueness among the group members is recognized and appreciated, thereby allowing the participants to grow and become involved throughout the training.

CHAPTER 2

Overview of Training

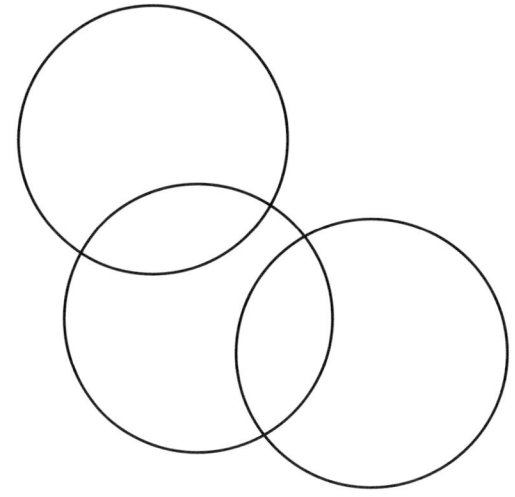

The objective of the Collaborative Training Model is to provide knowledge and skills to enhance confidence in teaching cultural competence in the field. Current models of field education are limited in helping field instructors directly address diversity issues with students (Armour et al., 2004). Field instructors are left, therefore, with the expectation that they should automatically know how to transfer knowledge about sensitive topics (such as cultural and social diversity) to their students. Field instructors may also be reticent to acknowledge their actual or presumed deficiency (Chan & Treacy, 1996; Garcia & Van Soest, 1999). This training seeks to empower field instructors by providing knowledge and skills, which include the ability to acknowledge more openly what they do not know.

Description of Training

The training that is described in this manual is intended to be adaptable for use by various types of institutions or schools, small and large, as well as schools in both rural and urban settings. Each institution or school that implements this model will have unique circumstances to be considered in the planning phase. In order to make the training model user friendly and adaptable, the training is described with one factor in mind—time.

The training can be implemented in two distinct designs:

- Full Design, which consists of 18 hours of training
- Modified Design, which consists of 14 hours of training

For both of these designs, the training can be delivered in two different ways:

- **Consecutively:** training days follow one after another without break or interruption
- **Intermittently:** training is conducted over a period of time, such as a month or a semester

The Full and Modified Designs delivered consecutively or intermittently result in seven different possible formats (see table below).

TABLE 1
Formats: Full and Modified Designs With Consecutive and Intermittent Schedules

SCHEDULE

MODEL	CONSECUTIVE	INTERMITTENT
Full Design: 18 hours	Format 1: 3 six-hour days	Format 2: 3 six-hour days
		Format 3: 6 three-hour days
Modified Design: 14 hours	Format 4: 2 days Day 1: 6 hours Day 2: 8 hours	Format 5: 2 days Day 1: 6 hours Day 2: 8 hours
	Format 6: 3 days Day 1: 4 hours Day 2: 5 hours Day 3: 5 hours	Format 7: 3 days Day 1: 4 hours Day 2: 5 hours Day 3: 5 hours

In all formats, the multiple themes of Relationship With Self, Relationship With Student Supervisee, and Relationship With Agency are addressed. Also, the six modules—and their specific exercises and lectures—are consistent throughout the seven different formats. As a result, the following components are *all* covered in each different schedule.

Theme: *Relationship With Self*
   Module 1: Welcoming Diversity in Self
              Introduction
              Exercise 1: Icebreaker
              Mini Lecture: Normalization of Anxiety
              Mini Lecture: Orientation to the Training
              Exercise 2: Weaving a Tapestry
              Exercise 3: Internalized Attitudes
              Exercise 4: Reclaiming Dignity and Honor
              Conclusion
              Reflecting Questions: Taking a Stand for Diversity
   Module 2: Taking a Stand for Diversity
              Introduction
              Round-Robin Responses
              Mini Lecture: Diving Deeper
              Exercise 1: Taking Power Back
              Exercise 2: Reevaluation
              Conclusion
              Reflecting Questions: Exploring Diversity in the Supervisory Relationship

Theme: *Relationship With Student Supervisee*
   Module 3: Exploring Diversity in the Supervisory Relationship
              Introduction and Round-Robin Responses
              Mini Lecture: Parallel Process
              Mini Lecture: Power
              Mini Lecture: Boundaries
              Exercise: Exploring Dilemmas
              Conclusion
              Reflecting Questions: Effecting Change in the Supervisory Relationship
   Module 4: Effecting Change in the Supervisory Relationship
              Introduction
              Round-Robin Responses
              Exercise 1: Role Playing
              Exercise 2: Group Consultation
              Exercise 3: Reconvened Role Playing
              Mini Lecture: Didactic Handout

Conclusion
Reflecting Questions: Diversity and Your Agency

Theme: *Relationship With Agency*
   Module 5: Diversity and Your Agency
        Introduction and Round-Robin Responses
        Mini Lecture: Cultural Competence Continuum
        Exercise: Agency Assessment
        Conclusion
        Reflecting Questions: Future Action
   Module 6: Future Action
        Introduction
        Round-Robin Responses
        Mini Lecture: Disempowerment
        Exercise: Roots of Disempowerment
        Mini Lecture: Changing Perspectives: The Agency as Your Client
        Conclusion

Reflecting Questions are located at strategic times and are aimed at integrating knowledge from previous sessions with preparation for upcoming ones. Debriefing and planning meetings for trainers are held to review progress and plan appropriate interventions. The 18-hour Full Design with the Intermittent Schedule is the only format that is research based and has shown to be effective. The 14-hour Modified Design is offered here as an alternative, given possible time constraints. See appendix A to review the seven different formats in detail.

Overall, the collaborative model is conceptualized as a developmental model, which provides field instructors with greater awareness in the following areas:

- Heritage and other issues and how they relate to diversity
- Learning how to use that awareness to improve teaching in the field
- Becoming more comfortable in being proactive as an advocate for change within their agencies

Likewise, becoming culturally competent takes time and involves a series of stages to achieve mastery (Hendricks, 2003).

CHAPTER 3

Training Team Meetings

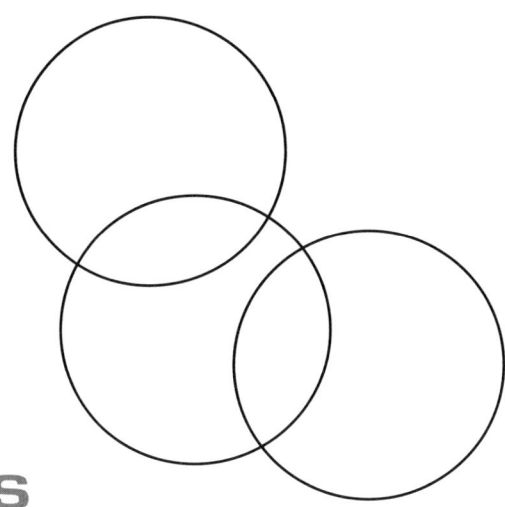

Debriefing and planning meetings are scheduled throughout the duration of the training regardless of the format used. Debriefing meetings are held after modules or sessions. They are used for trainers to share observations about individual participants and the group; identify themes, strengths, and possible areas of concern; and evaluate what was and was not effective in accomplishing the goals of a particular session. Individual needs of participants are recognized. For example, a participant may mention shame or defensiveness over having poor command of the English language. Another participant may make disparaging comments about growing up in an urban housing project. In response, trainers explore ways to address these specific needs during the next session or at some point in the training series.

Planning meetings are held before the training begins and before upcoming sessions. They are used to organize upcoming activities, develop exercises, delegate trainer responsibilities, and strategically assess areas for concentration. They ensure the continued focus on avoidance for trainers and participants, the articulation of anxiety, and the building of a supportive atmosphere for the development of skills. The time allotted for debriefing and planning meetings is dependent on the format used, namely, Full or Modified Designs, Consecutive or Intermittent Schedules.

Planning activities for the training include the following:

1. Define the learning objectives for each session or module.
2. Select the activities and mini lectures that will be used to meet the learning objectives.

3. Assign responsibility for the activities and mini lectures among members of the training team. The activities—all of which are contained in each module—include the following:
   - Introductions
   - Round-robin responses
   - Mini lectures
   - Objectives and instructions for exercises
   - Processing of exercises
   - Conclusions
   - Reflecting questions
4. Specify the time to be allotted to each activity or mini lecture.
5. Clarify tasks for the teaching assistant, such as copying materials, sending reminders, confirming the meeting location, and so on.

Trainers also need to develop role playing for supervision dyads between modules 3 and 4. Because the role playing is individualized and built on the pairing of differences among participants (age, ethnicity, gender, psychological temperament, agency clientele), it cannot be developed until the trainers have had the opportunity to get to know the participants through observation and interaction. Because the development of the role playing is an intricate process, trainers need to allot three to four hours for this process prior to Module 4 (Effecting Change in the Supervisory Relationship).

CHAPTER 4

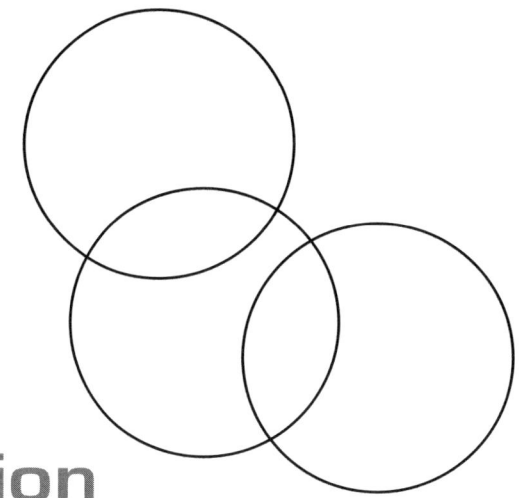

Planning and Preparation

The purpose of this section is to provide trainers with specific information as a guide to implementation of the training. Planning and preparation include the following:

1. Selection of participants and trainers
2. Administrative support
3. Location of training
4. Time frame
5. Practical arrangements
6. Trainer assignment
7. Follow-up
8. Issues and recommendations

Selection of Participants and Trainers

Construction of group membership should be guided by efforts to maximize cultural and social diversity. Diversity of both the field instructors and trainers can include race, ethnicity, national origin, gender, age, class, religion, sexual orientation, family structure, physical ability, and so forth. Diverse representation applies to the group members themselves as well as to the populations served by the participants' agencies. Diversity in participant and trainer professional interests and expertise also adds to the group experience. For example, trainers and participants might represent concentrations in clinical practice and administration and planning. When certain groups are not represented, trainers must initiate discussions about who is absent to help remind everyone that even in the social work profession, there are still serious inequities.

Trainers are encouraged to consider differences that may not be visible or obvious. The diversity within a given ethnic group, for example, may include:

- Identification as gay, lesbian, bisexual, or transgendered (GLBT)
- Use of English as a second language
- Length of time the family has been in this country
- Immigrations status

And, as indicated previously, other kinds of hidden diversities may include mental disabilities, class or class origins, religion, and so on. In areas that are ethnically homogeneous, it is essential for trainers to recognize the importance of intragroup differences.

Instead of offering this training to all field instructors, about 15 to 18 individuals are selected by the trainers to maximize diverse representation and are "invited" to participate in the training. The concept of an *invitation to participate* is intentional and results in the members of the group feeling valued and sharing a stake in the collaborative teaching/learning process. Participants are told that they have been selected because the trainers believe that they have a lot to offer the group. Experience with this model has validated the importance of carefully selecting and inviting participants to enhance their motivation to attend and provide them some leverage with their agencies for time off for the training.

As trainers consider this concept of *inviting* the participation of field instructors, a concern about being exclusionary may arise. In response to this possible issue, the following solutions are offered:

- The hope is that the training will be offered on an ongoing basis—not just once. The more often the training is made available, the more likely there will be broader representation of the field instructors from various communities and groups.
- There is a strategic opportunity to invite groups that have been traditionally underrepresented and seek out their active participation. This results in strategic inclusion.
- The increased number of field instructors who participate in the training will result in a larger pool of potential trainers for this model in the future.

Additionally, this invitation process does not preclude other people from expressing an interest in future participation. Moreover, the training is offered, in part, in appreciation for the service field instructors provide for the school. Participants are asked to commit to the entire training, rather than to move in and out of the group, for reasons of group cohesion and respect for the sensitivity of the topic.

Trainers include two or three representatives from the school of social work. The representatives may be field directors and coordinators, field staff, clinical faculty, or tenure/tenure-track faculty. Ideally, some of the trainers will have established strong relationships with field agencies over the years. At least one trainer should be skilled in clinical practice and one trainer should be representative of macropractice to assist in the application of learning to students' concentrations and varied field placements.

Administrative Support

An important member of the training team is the teaching assistant (TA). Besides assisting with the training, the TA provides feedback from the students' perspective to both trainers and participants. The TA is present at all planning, debriefing, and group sessions. The responsibilities of the TA include the following:

- Maintain communications with participants to remind them of upcoming sessions
- Help with group setup
- Send letters of appreciation to host agencies
- Provide feedback to trainers from the sessions
- Share ideas with the trainers to help them address group needs

Careful screening for this position is highly recommended. In those cases where a TA is not available, the training team may be able to identify a student and give credit for independent study or extra credit for a current course. Recent graduates or students from other disciplines also might be considered as possible volunteers for this project.

Location of Training

Training may be held at the university or college and/or at participants' agencies. The recommendation is to begin the training at the university or school and then move to other sites as desired. If the training begins at the academic institution, it affirms the notion that there is new knowledge to be gained by participating in the training and reinforces the school's commitment as a resource and partner in the ongoing effort to develop cultural competence. The advantage to using various sites, such as a specific agency, is that participants are able to tour each other's settings. Or, if the training is held in neighborhood centers within the community, participants are able to learn more about various communities in the area. If the training is held at participants' agencies, letters of appreciation signed by all trainers are sent to the various agency directors at the training's conclusion.

If lack of training space is an issue, the trainers are encouraged to look for other organizations with which to collaborate. Also, as noted above, neighborhood centers, libraries, and cultural centers may be considered and may possibly accentuate the central concept of cultural diversity.

Time Frame

The training should be planned well in advance to minimize conflicts with other university, agency, and/or community events. The realities of busy schedules, heavy professional demands on both educators and practitioners, and the inevitable glitches along the way are apt to compete for time and disrupt the reflective and soul-searching climate necessary for successful implementation of the Collaborative Training Model.

As noted previously, there are seven formats for offering this training. These seven formats fit into two schedules (Consecutive and Intermittent) and two designs (18-Hour Full Design and 14-Hour Modified Design). Depending on the format selected by the training team, the planning and debriefing meetings will vary. (See appendix A for more specifics on these different formats.)

In the Consecutive Schedule, the sessions follow one another without breaks. Consecutive sessions allow for an intense experience, increased retention of content, and continuity for the group process. Trainer debriefing meetings are held immediately after each session, as time allows. Trainer planning meetings will take place primarily before the training occurs and will be interspersed throughout, as time allows.

In the Intermittent Schedule, the sessions are distributed over a period of time, with each session separated from the next by a planned number of weeks. Spacing sessions allows the participants time to reflect, integrate, and apply what they are learning in the training. Trainer debriefing meetings are held immediately after each session. Trainer planning meetings are scheduled in between sessions. Refer to tables 7 and 8 in appendix A for a summary of other pros and cons of the Consecutive and Intermittent Schedules.

A final note: The articles that are annotated in appendix G are assigned during modules 1 and 2 or at the trainer's discretion depending on the format used.

Practical Arrangements

Practical arrangements may include parking, continuing education units (CEUs), money for refreshments, arranging for a group meeting room, and copying of handouts. Schools must be mindful of the need to prepare materials as needed before training sessions occur.

Trainer Assignments

This training uses two or three trainers. Each trainer takes primary responsibility for various activities based on his or her interests and expertise. Activities may include round-robin responses, mini lectures, exercises, or the processing of information at the conclusion of each module.

Follow-Up

The training team will want to consider the possibility of continuing the group beyond the designated time for the training session. The potential for strong group cohesiveness developing during the sessions is likely; therefore, the training group can be the basis for an ongoing group that meets periodically, such as every three or six months. The individuals can come together as a focus group and continue the discussions that began in the original training. This would be a voluntary component and perhaps will offer one of the participants the possibility for a leadership role in organizing and implementing the follow-up.

Group members may develop an electronic mailing list via the Web (e.g., Yahoo®) in order to keep the dialogue active among them. This online forum can provide a platform for challenges, suggestions, and recommended articles or books as well as give other field instructors the opportunity to sign up for future trainings.

Issues and Recommendations

As the trainers put this model into practice, there may be concerns about various aspects of planning and implementation. Examples of these concerns are trainer availability and expertise, time commitment for participants, homogeneity of the participants, and so forth. Table 2 lists these and other possible issues that may surface. Also listed are recommendations for possible solutions.

TABLE 2
Issues and Recommendations

ISSUES	RECOMMENDATIONS
Homogeneity of diversity in participants and size of participant pool	Expand to include non-field professionals and people from other schools/departments, namely, education, psychology, and nursing
	Include recent graduates
	Include other universities in a collaborative effort
	Expand concept of diversity to include non-visible differences, for example, class, religion, sexual orientation and gender identity, and mental disability
Trainer availability and expertise	Use one person from the university or college and others from the practice community
	Use individuals who have already gone through the training as participants
Lack of physical facility	Use agencies and community facilities, for example, cultural centers, libraries
Time commitment of trainers	Use non-work time or a combination of professional and personal time
	Teach as overload
Time commitment for participants	Explore modified modules included in appendix A of this manual
	Use nonwork time or a combination of professional and personal time
Lack of administrative support	Use a student and give credit for independent study, extra credit for a current course, use for research
	Use students from other disciplines
Transportation and travel	Explore modified modules included in this manual (see appendix A)
	Rotate location of training

CHAPTER 5

Implementation

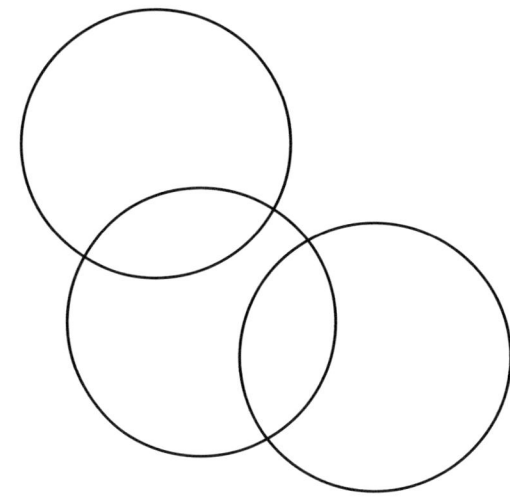

Procedural Overview

Common procedures are followed in each module. These procedures include:

1. Welcome/Introduction
2. Round-robin responses to reflecting questions
3. Mini lectures
4. Experiential exercises
5. Application to field education
6. Conclusion

Welcome/Introduction

Each group member is warmly welcomed at every session. Time is taken for informal greetings between group members and settling in prior to the formal training. Refreshments and coffee may be brought by the trainers and may include ethnic-specific treats. Ethnic-specific music can also be played as part of the welcome prior to beginning the first session. After the informal mingling, each module will open with a brief introduction, providing trainees with a basic overview of that day's session.

Round-Robin Responses to Reflecting Questions

After each module, participants are given Reflecting Questions to help them integrate knowledge and prepare for the upcoming session. Participants write answers to these Reflecting Questions and bring their answers to the next meeting.

Participants and trainers share selectively from their answers, which are provided in a round-robin format. This means that each person takes a turn giving an answer that person would like to share; a participant may pass if desired. Trainers keep the discussion flowing from one participant to another, gathering answers, taking only minimal time for discussion. After each person has the opportunity to speak once, the floor is open for a discussion by the entire group. Participants can offer feedback to each other as well as observations about common themes and new insights.

During the sharing, trainers listen for themes, especially noting areas of discomfort or resistance, and identify opportunities for naming the elephant in the room. Participants are asked to turn in their answers at the end of the sharing time. Trainers use information gained from participants' answers in planning for future sessions.

Mini Lectures

Each module includes brief, thought-provoking mini lectures on relevant topics related to the experience of self-awareness, being direct with students, or addressing barriers to help agencies become more culturally competent. Mini lectures usually precede or follow exercises and are used to deepen the participants' experience. Trainers may decide to add mini lectures on particular topics based on participants' responses to Reflecting Questions or issues that surface during previous modules.

Experiential Exercises

Experiential exercises are used in each module to generate material for discussion or teach abstract principles. Reflection and discussion of the participants' experience allows individuals to share reactions as well as learn from and support each other in recognizing patterns, such as the anxiety and human tendency to avoid discomfort in becoming more culturally competent. Although the focus is on each participant's experience, the process is interactional. For example, trainers may ask questions, make comments about what has been said, draw connections to previously made statements, or offer ideas related to the topic being covered. This open interaction helps participants feel understood, challenged, and valued because they receive a personal response to what they have shared. Open interaction also models for participants the attitude and behaviors for engaging with their social work students who come to work in their agencies.

Application to Field Education

Participants are challenged to examine and apply their experiences from each module to field teaching. Application to field may occur during participants' responses to Reflecting Questions, after experiential exercises, and at the conclusion of each module. Trainers frequently initiate discussions or make comments as opportunities occur for the transfer of knowledge from the participants' personal associations to a professional context. Participants are also reminded regularly of the significance of the parallel process with their students.

Conclusion

Each module closes with a round-robin question to participants about their experience. This procedure also allows the trainers to add their personal experiences of the group and to underline themes that can serve as anchors for the group. Reflecting Questions are distributed at the end of each module. Participants are also invited to share any final impressions, comments, or suggestions based on their experience of the module. This feedback is incorporated into planning for the next module. Information about subsequent sessions, including date, time, location, parking instructions, and any other pertinent details is discussed.

PART 2

Relationship With Self

Focus: The focus of these modules is to enhance self-awareness related to diversity and articulate concerns about teaching cultural competence in field.

Objectives:

1. Enhance awareness of and pride in one's own cultural heritage
2. Build community through an appreciation of the similarities and differences among participants

Module 1: Welcoming Diversity in Self
- Introduction
- Exercise 1: Icebreaker
- Mini Lecture: Normalization of Anxiety
- Mini Lecture: Orientation to the Training
- Exercise 2: Weaving a Tapestry
- Exercise 3: Internalized Attitudes
- Exercise 4: Reclaiming Dignity and Honor
- Conclusion
- Reflecting Questions: Taking a Stand for Diversity

Module 2: Taking a Stand for Diversity
- Introduction
- Round-Robin Responses
- Mini Lecture: Diving Deeper
- Exercise 1: Taking Power Back
- Exercise 2: Reevaluation
- Conclusion
- Reflecting Questions: Exploring Diversity in the Supervisory Relationship

CHAPTER 6

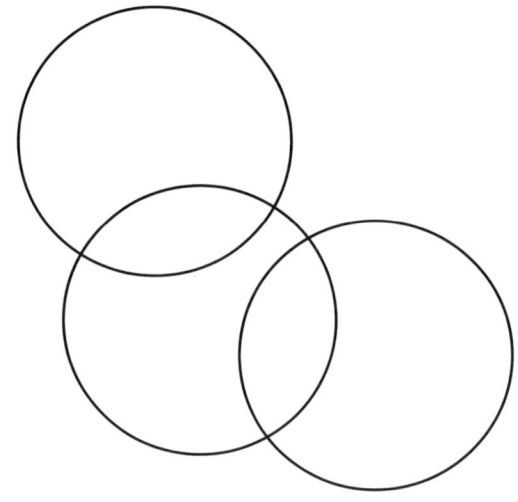

Module 1
Welcoming Diversity in Self

Introduction

Introduce yourselves and welcome the participating field instructors enthusiastically. Explain how the participants were invited to attend this training. Emphasize that the participants are valued for their contributions to students and their dedication to excellence in professional social work education. Also acknowledge that participants may have experience with diversity training. Note that participants may not have been satisfied with the quality of the experience. State that the diversity training is provided to enhance their teaching of social work students in the field.

Exercise 1 Icebreaker

Objective

The icebreaker exercise is a structured way for participants to introduce themselves to the group. It also helps participants experience the "richness in the room" from the diversity among themselves and the trainers.

Instructions

Demonstrate this exercise first and then ask each participant to introduce himself or herself in the following manner:

WELCOMING DIVERSITY IN SELF

EXERCISE 1 Icebreaker

1. Identify self by name, agency, experience in supervision, and interest in the training topic.

2. Share (if comfortable) ethnic and/or religious or spiritual heritage or other social groups you belong to. For example: "I am a refugee from Bosnia. I grew up in a war zone before coming to the United States with my family in 1995."

3. Describe a family-of-origin tradition that reflects your heritage or a meaningful tradition that you have created since leaving your family of origin. For example: "I am Mexican American from a large, extended family, and every fall we gather at my grandmother's to make tamales for the Christmas season. Making tamales is labor intensive, but there is always a sense of community, caring, and laughter."

Processing

After all participants have introduced themselves, ask them to discuss their reactions to the exercise and what they learned about each other. A round-robin format is used. During this first group exercise, you may need to be more active in modeling the responses from an affirmative perspective. For example, you may take the lead after everyone has had the opportunity to introduce himself or herself, by saying something like:

> This group is more wonderfully diverse than even we knew. I notice that we are all in different places regarding awareness of our heritage. We believe that by knowing and taking pride in one's own heritage, it is easier to appreciate the differences in groups other than our own. I am impressed with the level of sharing and feel fortunate to be working with all of you.

Be authentic and emphasize the positive as specifically as possible. Some participants whose sense of ethnic or religious tradition has been lost may feel some awkwardness as they struggle to identify the exact origins of their culture. Help participants to see that many students may also struggle with the mistaken idea that they do not have a culture because they are just "plain vanilla American." Point out that this exercise can also be used with students to help them begin thinking about who they are in more depth, and stimulate their appreciation of different groups and traditions.

Ask the following questions to help participants process the exercise:

1. Did you recognize any themes or learn something you didn't know before?

2. What was difficult or frustrating for you in this experience?

3. What was most enjoyable or important to you?

4. Would you use this exercise or some variation of it with students or in your agency?
5. What would you like to change about the exercise or your participation?

Mini Lecture Normalization of Anxiety

Objective

Introduce participants to the central idea of everyone in the group being a work in progress—and anxiety is part of that process.

Instructions

Initiate the idea that addressing social and cultural diversity is anxiety provoking for both participants and trainers. If the anxiety is not made overt and its origin understood, the tendency, according to Pinderhughes (1989), is to use superiority as a solution to discomfort about difference. At the end of the mini lecture place a small statue of an elephant on a table where everyone can see it. The elephant is brought to each of the other sessions.

Content

The recognition of social and cultural differences and the related issues of power, privilege, and oppression are anxiety provoking for all of us, including the trainers. For example, our decision to intentionally examine these issues through offering this training creates anxiety. Although there are many reasons for this anxiety, one of the biggest contributors is our belief that there is a right way to "do diversity." That is, someone knows better than we do. Someone knows more than we do. The truth of the matter is that no one has *the* answer, but we keep thinking that someone does. We assume that because someone has experienced discrimination, is African American, disabled, or speaks Spanish or is older and therefore wiser, that person must know more than we do. The larger reality is that there are *no experts,* and there is no one right way. Everyone has ideas about what is wrong or what might help to figure out the diversity puzzle, but *no one has the answer*. We're just all in this together struggling to figure it out. Yet as long as we believe someone else knows more, we hold back waiting for the answer or become cautious because we want to do it right. So, as trainers, we constantly have to remind ourselves that

- There are no experts.
- There is no end stage of "having arrived" in relation to cultural competence.
- We are all works in progress.

Another problem is that when we feel anxiety or discomfort, we think something is wrong. We don't realize that the anxiety we are feeling is a natural and *inherent* part of dealing with diversity issues. It comes with the territory. The consequence of not recognizing this basic connection is that we back off when we feel the discomfort, never recognizing that the discomfort does *not* mean something is wrong. It might even mean that something is right because the discomfort is a signal we are approaching anxiety-laden material. That is, we are in the territory we should be in. Once we understand that anxiety or discomfort is not indicative of a problem or attached to doing something wrong, it is easier to accept the discomfort that accompanies dealing with differentness and inequity. Indeed, we realize that the real challenge is whether we are willing to tolerate discomfort rather than avoid it. It is essential that our capacity to tolerate discomfort becomes an indicator of progress rather than a negative and undesirable state.

Last, we need to acknowledge that we often act as if there is a choice about whether to approach social and cultural differences and related social inequities. Or we act as if we have a choice about whether to grow the tolerance for our own discomfort that is intrinsic to diversity work. We need to recognize that the concept of choice is an illusion. Once we can accept that diversity issues belong to all of us and that we are all in the struggle together, discomfort becomes an inherent part of the journey rather than something to avoid.

To represent the work we have to do, we present this small statue of an elephant as a symbol of the idiom, "the elephant in the room," which is typically ignored or avoided whenever uncertainty and/or anxiety prevails.

Mini Lecture **Orientation to the Training**

Objective

Provide the goals, assumptions, and structure for the training model and establish rules for group safety.

Instructions

Describe the three organizing themes of the training, which are Relationship With Self, Relationship With Student Supervisee, and Relationship With Agency, the cornerstone concepts, and the need for a commitment to confidentiality.

Content

This training is divided into three parts: The field instructor's relationship with himself or herself, the field instructor's relationship with the student supervisee, and the field instructor's relationship with the agency where he or she works.

MINI LECTURE Orientation to the Training

Each of these areas has its own challenges and creates discomfort and the tendency to avoid those topics or behaviors that produce the discomfort. For example, if I'm a heterosexual male and unfamiliar with gay culture, I may minimize the discomfort I feel inside myself by keeping a distance with an openly gay coworker. If I know my female student is evangelical, and I have beliefs and judgments about devout Christians or the promulgation of Christianity, I may avoid dealing with the topic of her religion or limit exploring how the student manages her religious beliefs when she works with Hmong or Serbian refugees. If I work in an agency that has few if any staff of color, I may remain silent about the Whiteness around me because I believe that my commenting would be in vain or could make for trouble. Our goal in this training is to give you tools to intervene on the discomfort in each of these areas—relationship with yourself, your student supervisee, and your agency—so that you can be more culturally competent and effective as a field instructor with your students. Concomitantly, your ability to intervene on your own discomfort will help your students be less avoidant in dealing with the differences between themselves and their clients. The sequencing of the content is deliberate. We view striving for cultural competence as a development process that must start with enhancing awareness and pride in one's own heritage as well as the effects of privilege and oppression in this society (Pinderhughes, 1989).

This training rests on five cornerstone concepts.

- Collaboration between the university and the practice community
- Collaboration between trainers and participants
- Normalizing anxiety and avoidance
- Celebrating differences
- Skill development for dealing directly with differences

Collaboration Between the University and the Practice Community

This training is built on a partnership between the university and the practice community. For example, we know that you have professional struggles and obstacles to dealing with issues of social and cultural diversity in your agencies that can inform us and what we need to address in this training We also have some of the pieces of the diversity puzzle (Walters et al., 1998). We therefore have structured this training as intentionally interactive. Our goal is that this open partnership between us will maximize the possibility for mutual trust and growth.

Collaboration Between Trainers and Participants

We view all of us as works in progress. That is, we *all* have an ethical commitment, as social workers, to engage continually in the process of becoming more culturally competent. We will join with you in telling stories about ourselves—stories about where we fumbled and stories about where something seemed to work. Although our roles may be different, we are alike in making this journey because this process for all of us is never ending. There are no graduates in cultural competence if social workers live according to social work values.

Normalizing Anxiety and Avoidance

No one can sincerely engage in the struggle to become more culturally competent without experiencing some anxiety in the process. Some of the triggers for anxiety are:

- Fear of unintentionally offending in attempting to discuss or identify diversity issues
- Feelings of guilt
- Painful experiences
- Fear of exposing your hidden biases
- Dissonance between beliefs and actions

As we discussed earlier, normalizing anxiety and the human tendency to avoid what is uncomfortable or anxiety producing is a central organizing theme throughout the training. We will bring the elephant to each session and place it in plain sight, so that everyone has a visual reminder of the human tendency to avoid what is uncomfortable. We hope that your ability to own and discuss candidly the anxiety involved in diversity work can eventually be seen as an indication of your sincerity and motivation to grow in becoming culturally competent.

Celebrating Differences

In the mainstream culture of the United States, the values of rugged individualism and competition, the domination of dualistic thinking, and ethnocentrism are inescapable influences in shaping attitudes toward and approaches to diversity. Moreover, since we are taught to think of diversity as creating problems, we tend to react in ways that ignore or minimize the differences between us. This point is illustrated by such statements as the following:

- "I don't have any culture; I am just American."
- "We are all human, so why don't we emphasize how we are all alike instead of talking about how we are different?"

MINI LECTURE Orientation to the Training

Celebrating differences includes first recognizing the range of differences that constitute social and cultural diversity. Culture—as it is used in this training model—is broadly defined to include ethnicity, race, national origin, social class, age, sexual orientation, gender identity, religion, family structure, and mental or physical disability (NASW, 2001). This model encourages the expanded awareness of "hidden" differences, such as use of language, immigration status, and skin color variation. Other less than obvious differences could include mental disabilities, birth order, and sexual orientation and gender identity. The model also recognizes the concept of multiple identities (Van Soest, 2004).

In addition, celebrating differences includes the sometimes painful process of becoming aware of the many ways all of us are affected by unearned privilege and oppression in this society (Gutiérrez & Nagda, 1996; Hyde & Ruth, 2002; Lum, 1999; Miller et al., 2004; Van Soest, 2004). Indeed, because we all have multiple social identities, people are both targets of oppression and agents of oppression (Bell, 1997). In this training model, privilege is defined as unearned entitlements for a certain group and exclusion of others, such as limited employment opportunities for older people. Privilege also includes conferred dominance, which gives one group power over another, such as people who are abled in contrast to people with disabilities (McIntosh, 1993).

We hope that this training will help make overt the internalization of beliefs that result in being alienated or ashamed of one's own culture. This hope is based on the belief that we are better able to welcome and celebrate differences if these differences are positively reinforced, and people are encouraged to recognize that they take pride in the characteristics that define their own cultural groups and heritage (Pinderhughes, 1989).

Skill Development for Dealing Directly With Differences

At the University of Texas at Austin, a survey that was given to field instructors and their students found that both groups had difficulty directly addressing diversity issues in supervision despite exposure to ethnically diverse client populations (Bain & Garcia, 1999). This training uses the concept of parallel process with field instructors to model what you need to do with students. Specifically, our goal is to give you tools to deal *more directly* with issues of diversity in your supervisory relationships with your social work students (Torres & Jones, 1997). Students then can mirror the process with their clients by drawing on the internalized experience they have had in supervision with you (Doehrman, 1976). It is our hope that giving you tools will help decrease anxiety and raise your confidence in your ability to address issues of social and cultural diversity with students. By *directly*, we mean the ability to be appropriately open and candid about differences. We also recognize that some cultures do not value directness. We therefore want you to be aware of the mores within your own cultural context and derive strategies for addressing a student's learning needs that include sensitivity to a variety of communication styles.

Because the manifestation of avoidance is highly individualized and varies by person and subject matter, we use an open-ended planning process to tailor the training to your needs, experiences, and your comfort or discomfort with the issues. That means that even though the training follows a semistructured agenda, we may make changes along the way to help engage you at a personal level and allow the material to be more relevant and meaningful.

In order to make this training safe for all participants, we ask you to commit to the following rules:

- Sharing with the group is voluntary. You must make a personal decision about what to share and how much to share.
- You must share only your own experience of the training outside the group and do not discuss anyone else's experience or issues.
- You must listen respectfully to your colleagues whether or not you agree.
- You must keep any discussion of agency concerns within the group.

Exercise 2 Weaving a Tapestry

Objective

This exercise is designed to help participants become aware of diversity and the feelings associated with being identified with specific groups.

Instructions

Introduce the idea that diversity training is like weaving a tapestry. Although this metaphor highlights the reality that people bring together different colors, contours, and textures to the experience, it is also important to remember that people are joined, in part, by the common experience of hurt embedded in messages about the groups individuals belong to. In the following exercise, bring these hurtful messages out in the open and help participants to leave their negative effects behind. This exercise also helps individuals become more aware of their hurt in order to sensitize them to the hurts of others.

For this exercise, lead participants through the following steps:

1. Take three deep breaths, come completely into the room. Silently name three to five groups you identify with. Your groups can be defined on the

EXERCISE 3 Internalized Attitudes

basis of ethnicity, religion, class, age, gender identity, sexual orientation, geographic location, professional identification, interests, and so on.

2. Write down the names of the groups you identify with. (Trainers give examples to the participants. "Some of the groups you might identify with are stepmother, African American, social worker, suicide survivor, refugee, child of foster care system, Christian.")

3. Choose a partner. Share your list and what it means to you to belong to each group.

Processing

Ask for volunteers to share their lists with the group. Comment on the diversity of groups represented. Then ask the following questions:

1. What happened to you as you thought about the various groups you belong to?
2. What are your impressions about demands, challenges, and/or expectations placed on you as a result of being a member of certain groups?
3. What thoughts or feelings came up when you listened to your partner list his or her groups?
4. What else would you like to explore related to your groups? Other groups?
5. Consider how membership in your groups may contribute to your being privileged in some way. What is it like to think of yourself as privileged? What is it like to think of yourself or others as having unmerited privilege?

Exercise 3 Internalized Attitudes

Objective

The purpose of this exercise is to help access internalized negative attitudes about the groups we belong to.

Instructions

Prior to asking participants to engage in the following exercise, model it for the group members. This modeling gives trainers an opportunity to self-disclose the difficulties experienced while doing this specific exercise, but also reassures the group that the more authentic their responses are, the more they will benefit from the exercise. For example, trainers might state the following: "I am Chinese. Chinese are Communists; they only value sons and show no feelings." Afterward, lead participants through the following steps:

1. Think about each of the groups that have been identified as your groups.

EXERCISE 4 Reclaiming Dignity and Honor

2. Write at least one negative message that you have heard from your family or others about each group. Try not to censor or edit your responses in any way. What you write is not a reflection of what you believe to be true now. Rather, it is an indication of hurts likely accumulated from people from outside your groups.

3. After participants have completed their lists, choose a new partner. Take turns reading your lists to each other.

Processing

Ask for volunteers to share their lists with the group. During the sharing, comment verbally and give nonverbal cues while paying particular attention to each participant's honesty and courage. To encourage further dialogue, ask the following questions:

1. What feelings came up for you as you wrote down the negative messages about your groups?
2. What happened when you heard your partner or others in the group read their lists?
3. If you heard anyone else say something about your group, how are you likely to respond?
4. If anyone else gave a negative message about one of your partner's groups or someone else's groups in this training, how would you respond?
5. What are the themes in these messages?

Ask participants to exchange their lists with negative messages with another group member and then request that participants shred the lists into tiny pieces. Alternatively, a group member can elect to keep or shred his or her own list. After the lists have been shredded, bring closure to the ritual by saying the following: "In this small symbolic way, we hope to move further away from the hurt that these old messages may have caused."

Exercise 4 Reclaiming Dignity and Honor

Objective

The purpose of this exercise is to help participants develop a sense of pride in their own groups.

Instructions

Ask participants to embrace their own heritage by making positive associations

EXERCISE 4 Reclaiming Dignity and Honor

with the groups they belong to. Also ask group members to recognize the strength and beauty in the groups other training members belong to.

Lead the participants through the following steps:

1. Revisit the groups you belong to.
2. Write down a positive characteristic or contribution from each group. Think of attributes that are sources of pride for you.
3. Stay with the same partner that you had for the previous exercise. Take turns reading your lists to each other.

Processing

Ask for volunteers to share their lists with the group. As participants share, make large posters of sources of pride so they are displayed and honored (or write them on a board). During the discussion, ask the following questions:

1. How did you experience this exercise compared to the previous two exercises?
2. How do we recognize that sometimes we feel badly about some of the things that members of our groups do or say, and yet let ourselves feel proud of who we are as members of those same groups? Give an example: "As a gay Black man, I feel bad about other gay men who stay closeted and ashamed of my brothers who have unprotected sex with numerous lovers, but I feel proud of our achievements, of people like the writer James Baldwin who is 'out,' and of our ability to change the rules about same-sex marriage."
3. What else do you want to explore about your own cultural heritage?
4. Are you curious about the negative and positive messages of groups other than your own?

Conclusion

Ask participants to identify and reflect on what they experienced during the group. For example, "When were you most uncomfortable? What did you do about it, if anything?" Offer encouragement and praise to those participants who risked themselves and "owned" areas of improvement in order to become more culturally competent teachers. Also, balance support with challenge by pointing out that waiting for the right moment to discuss diversity issues may be avoidance and can be used to justify not acting. Participants are encouraged to see that their discomfort is related to their fears that they will somehow be offensive or make racist blunders or be perceived as disrespectful. Reassure participants that this anxiety is normal; it is tied to the myth that there is one right way to deal with diversity issues. They are reminded that this training's purpose is to help them tolerate this discomfort so that their anxiety will not get in the way of their ability to address diversity issues directly with students. Trainers also point out specific moments in which participants learned something new or were inspired to think in a new way. Reinforce the concept that the need to become more culturally competent teachers is not optional; it demands courage and a lifelong commitment from everyone.

At the conclusion, hand out the first set of Reflecting Questions. Participants are told that the purpose of these questions is to help them think about themselves and the influences and challenges that have affected their attitudes toward their own group and groups other than their own. In answering the Reflecting Questions, they are also asked to discuss their misgivings about teaching cultural competence in the field. Remind the participants that they will receive Reflecting Questions at every module's end as homework for the next session. Responses to questions are turned in at the following session without names.

Reflecting Questions: Taking a Stand for Diversity

1. Share one experience of working with a supervisee who challenged or stimulated you to think differently about your own or another group.

2. Share some of your thoughts and feelings (including your fears and misgivings) about teaching cultural competency in the field.

3. Briefly write about one person or experience that helped you to feel good about yourself as a member of a particular group.

4. Identify a person from your group whom you most admire and indicate the reason for your admiration.

5. Provide comments, thoughts, and ideas that you would like to share regarding this topic or your experience in field.

Questions 1 and 2 are essential.

CHAPTER 7

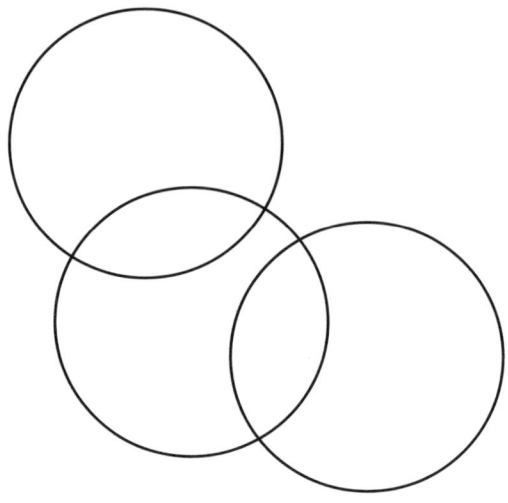

Module 2
Taking a Stand for Diversity

Introduction
The purpose of Module 2 is to enrich and deepen awareness about diversity and the pain that comes with discrimination and prejudice. Effective diversity training is more than an intellectual exercise; it allows feelings to surface and helps participants move beyond their discomfort to acknowledge their own pain and have compassion for the pain of others. Without personal sharing of some of these experiences, awareness of and sensitivity to diversity remains an intellectual exercise. Avoidance of the pain is another form of ignoring the elephant in the room.

Round-Robin Responses
Welcome the participants. Then review ground rules about confidentiality. Participants are reminded that they have choice about what and how much to share in the group. Then they are invited to share responses to the Reflecting Questions. Questions 1 and 2 elicit participants' struggles with students and themselves as field instructors about diversity issues. Questions 3 and 4 help participants describe group membership from a place of pride. During the sharing of the answers, take note of the following:

- Content of the sharing
- Mood of the sharing
- Dynamics related to who shares what

- Level of commitment and thoughtfulness of the responses
- Group's responses to listening to each other

Pay particular attention to participants' fears and hesitancy to initiate discussions with students. Respond to these concerns by reminding participants of the significance of parallel process: Students will imitate the field instructor and avoid with clients the material that is avoided in supervision. Also, help field instructors move past their paralysis by giving the following suggestions:

- Join with students as learners and allies in the diversity struggle.
- Admit mistakes.
- Notify students of the commitment by field instructors to pursue taboo topics with them.
- Clarify feelings generated by issues of social injustice, such as shame, hurt, and anger, in order to stop the students' suppression of unacceptable emotion.

Mini Lecture **Diving Deeper**

Objective

Reinforce the importance of the participants being active learners.

Content

Diving deeper means becoming aware of the many ways each person is affected by privilege and oppression in this society. Shared pain serves as a bridge to one another that furthers connection and comfort.

Before diving deeper, we want to remind you about the relationship between this training and the social work values embodied in the NASW *Standards for Cultural Competence in Social Work Practice* (2001), namely, dignity and worth of the person, social justice, and competence. To further the development of cultural competence, however, we must remember the following:

- Any diversity training must start with self-examination.
- There are no perfect specimens or graduates of culturally competent practice.
- Becoming more self-aware may be uncomfortable and may never be completed.

The consensus of the past was to minimize differences and "whitewash" people based on the assumption that individuals were all human with common human needs. Today, we have moved from the melting-pot philosophy of assimilation into the White middle class as the preferred way to handle cultural differences. In its

38 TAKING A STAND FOR DIVERSITY

EXERCISE 1 Taking Power Back

place, we now work with the metaphor of a salad that consists of unique social and cultural differences. We continue to use the salad metaphor today to remind us to value and celebrate the differences among us. However, the larger reality is that multiculturalism and issues of social justice are intertwined (Giroux, 1996). These same social and cultural differences that we strive to value and celebrate also have assigned meanings and socially ascribed statuses that reflect attitudes and inequities, further stereotypes, and produce pain. Homophobia, sexual harassment, workplace discrimination, and hate crimes are just a few examples of the link between social and cultural diversity and power, privilege, and oppression.

Many of us have experiences both as targets of oppression and inadvertent agents of oppression (Bell, 1997). The private pain that we share about these experiences creates internal devastation, shame, and impotence. That pain has value and importance, however, because it is a potential bridge to each other. When we can acknowledge our own pain and that of others who are different from us, we end up more connected and can find comfort in each other. The group exercises you will experience is this session, and throughout the training, reflect this philosophy and our belief that to be effective, you, as participants, must be active learners whose hearts and feelings are also engaged in the experiential opportunities.

Exercise 1 Taking Power Back

Objective

The purpose of this exercise is to help participants feel empowered to move past the conditions, for example, oppression and stigma, that silence them, "find their voice," and begin to advocate for the groups they belong to.

Instructions

Lead the group in the following steps:

1. Recall some of the groups you belong to.
2. Select a group you would like to advocate for.
3. Choose a partner and share the selected group. Your partner begins the exercise by stating a negative stereotype about the group. You have three opportunities to respond.
4. Your partner writes down your responses and tells you which response was the most effective in correcting the stereotype and why. Then it is your partner's turn to select a group and follow the same procedure.

Become partners with another trainer to model the exercise. Each one of you (the trainers) will select a group you belong to, for example, Jews. Ask your fellow trainer to repeat a negative stereotypical message about that group such as "Jews are cheap, stingy, and loud." Then you will counter with responses to the stated stereotype. Some possible responses might be, "What a stupid thing to say" or "I'm curious where that idea comes from for you. Have you had some experiences in which people who are Jewish and important to you were miserly?"

Processing

Ask volunteers to share effective responses. Express your encouragement by clapping or making supportive comments. If time is an issue, you may opt to limit the processing to the first three essential questions and consider the others optional.

1. What feelings came up when you gave the negative message? How were you able to manage them?
2. What factors should be considered in deciding whether and how to respond?
3. What would you have done differently to respond effectively to the stereotype about your group and why?
4. When you heard your partner say something negative about your group, what was your reaction? To what extent was your reaction authentic, that is, the way you believe you would have reacted in any other circumstance? How was it different?
5. What was most difficult about formulating your responses to the negative stereotypes?
6. What was it like to make a stereotypic statement? What was it like to receive your partner's response? How could he or she have advocated for himself or herself and maximized your ability to consider the feedback?
7. How do you feel about your group and your responses now?

Normalize how difficult it is to hear negative stereotypes about those groups we belong to, for example, being Native American or being a child of an incarcerated parent. Help participants identify what they did to advocate effectively for their group.

Exercise 2 **Reevaluation**

Objective

The purpose of this exercise is for participants to rewrite their negative experiences by increasing options for how they might respond.

40 TAKING A STAND FOR DIVERSITY

EXERCISE 2 Reevaluation

Instructions

Trainers should be alert to the potential for participants to be more emotional during this exercise. It is important to remind participants that they get to choose whether to disclose and how much to disclose. If emotions surface, it is important to acknowledge the pain and to remind participants that feeling the pain is a courageous choice toward healing, moving on, and connecting with others. Use the break to check in with individuals who have expressed a lot of emotion during the exercise, so you can assess if any further processing is necessary.

If time is an issue, the small-group sharing can be eliminated, and trainers may select one or two volunteers to share their stories with the entire group.

Lead the group in the following steps:

1. Write your name and "Yes" on a slip of paper if you are willing to share a personal experience of discrimination or prejudice in a small group (5 to 6 participants).

2. Select an experience that isn't too raw, for example, a situation you have sufficiently healed from to be able to tell your story without the risk of feeling too exposed. Please also indicate the nature of the incident, such as job discrimination because of being deaf, name calling because of being from the Middle East, false accusation because of a group affiliation such as HIV positive *because of* being gay, and so on. Do not volunteer stories that are intensely intimate, such as being a victim of sexual abuse or stories that describe situations you are actively recovering from.

3. Place the slip of paper in a basket or hat. The trainers will select stories from the hat to be told in small groups. The slips of paper are collected, sorted out by the trainers (possibly during a break), and selected for small-group sharing.

4. Separate into small groups with one or two volunteers per group to share their stories. Alternatively, if not enough participants volunteer to tell their stories, trainers may invite participants to share personal experiences that have increased their sensitivity to the effects of oppression in this society.

5. Volunteers share their stories of oppression or discrimination and their impact on their lives during the past and present. Volunteers are also given an opportunity to say now to the person who was hurtful what they were not able to say or do then. As a part of the process, trainers may give suggestions about what to say in order to promote healing or moving beyond the pain generated by the incident being discussed.

6. One or two volunteers are solicited from the entire group and asked to tell their personal stories about prejudice or discrimination. A trainer stands beside each of the volunteers for support while they share their stories. Although time limits this exercise to several volunteers, trainers may relate to the volunteers from their own backgrounds and become reflective about their own experiences.

7. After the story of oppression or discrimination has been told, trainers ask the volunteer what he or she would like to hear from the group in order to continue to grow and heal. At this point, the rest of the group is asked to respond.

During this exercise, offer verbal acknowledgment for the courage of the volunteer and empathy for his or her past hurts. Model giving supportive feedback and invite the entire group to give constructive responses as well. Unlike some other exercises in Modules 1 and 2, facilitators do not model this particular excercise. Also, provide ample permission for participants to decline sharing in the large group.

Processing

Ask the following questions after the reevaluation exercise:

1. What does the group recognize as evidence of resiliency and empowerment in the volunteers?
2. What were the themes in the stories?
3. What facilitates recovery from prejudicial hurts and the impact of oppression?
4. How do vulnerable people find their voice?
5. What have these stories stirred in you? How do you plan to go from here in terms of cultivating your own cultural competency?

Trainers share thoughts and feelings about the power of unearned privilege, prejudice, and the resiliency of the human spirit. Trainers along with the entire group acknowledge the volunteers for their courageous participation.

Conclusion

Ask participants to identify and reflect on what they experienced in the session with questions such as "What was the most important thing that happened for you today?" or "What made you most uncomfortable?" Then ask participants to apply what they learned in the session to field instruction by posing the following questions:

1. Can you use these exercises as a tool with your students? Or have they given you ideas for developing your own exercises to facilitate their learning about differences?
2. What is the implication for your teaching if you consider the parallel process and invite students into the struggle?
3. Is there anything you would change in your previous work with supervisees given what you experienced today?

Participants commonly realize that they need to engage students on a more personal and vulnerable level. This realization creates anxiety because they might not know how to do it. Help participants move past their resistance by giving the following suggestions (as noted earlier in this module):

- Join with students as learners and allies in the diversity struggle.
- Admit mistakes.
- Notify students of the commitment by field instructors to pursue taboo topics with them.
- Clarify feelings generated by recognition of social injustices, such as shame, hurt, and anger, in order to stop the students' suppression of unacceptable emotions.

Trainers share impressions of the group from a positive perspective. Verbally review and reinforce when participants took risks, supported one another, or worked respectfully with differences.

Distribute the Reflecting Questions, the handout on Racial Identity Development (see appendix H), and Recommended Articles (see appendix G) to participants. Remind the group that the purpose of assigning questions is to help them focus on themselves and diversity issues between training sessions. This concludes Module 2. Now the training shifts from an emphasis on the Relationship With Self to the Relationship With Student Supervisee. The Reflecting Questions indicate this shift in emphasis and will be used to inspire sharing and discussion in Module 3. Remind participants that the Reflecting Questions are to be turned in at the beginning of the next session without their names.

Reflecting Questions:
Exploring Diversity in the Supervisory Relationship

1. What differences between you and your student supervisee are most comfortable to deal with as a normal part of developing the supervisory relationship? What have you discovered to be the most effective way to deal with these differences?

2. Which differences between field instructor and student are more difficult for you, and what questions do you have about how to deal with these differences in supervision?

3. Identify one memorable negative experience that you have had as either a supervisee or a supervisor. In hindsight, did social or cultural differences between supervisor/supervisee, for example, class, age, gender, race, or ethnicity, contribute to the difficulty? What did you learn from that experience that relates to your ability to supervise now?

4. How does the handout on Racial Identity Development apply to you and your supervisees?

PART 3

Relationship With Student Supervisee

Focus: The focus of these sessions is on developing skills to address diversity issues in the supervisory relationship.

Objectives:
1. Enhance ability to respond directly to interpersonal differences in the supervisory and worker-client relationships
2. Develop the use of parallel process as a conceptual tool to assess field instructor and student avoidance
3. Increase application of the supervisory relationship as a medium for interventions that are transferable to worker-client relationships

Module 3: Exploring Diversity in the Supervisory Relationship
    Introduction and Round-Robin Responses
    Mini Lecture: Parallel Process
    Mini Lecture: Power
    Mini Lecture: Boundaries
    Exercise: Exploring Dilemmas
    Conclusion
    Reflecting Questions: Effecting Change in the Supervisory Relationship

Module 4: Effecting Change in the Supervisory Relationship
    Introduction

        Round-Robin Responses
        Exercise 1: Role Playing
        Exercise 2: Group Consultation
        Exercise 3: Reconvened Role Playing
        Mini Lecture: Didactic Handout
        Conclusion
        Reflecting Questions: Diversity and Your Agency

Module 3 is used to gather information on how avoidance is manifested in the supervisory relationship. It also introduces the following concepts:

- Parallel process
- Personal engagement and directness
- Role power
- Boundary setting in addressing social and cultural diversity issues

These concepts are presented through mini lectures and in response to participants' stories about dilemmas in dealing with interpersonal differences. As you apply these concepts to the participants' material, participants become unsettled because of the implicit demand for risking new behaviors.

Module 4 is used to develop skills in recognizing the parallel process, initiating direct and personal interaction with the student, and following a protocol for case presentations that increases the student's effectiveness with diverse clients. Trainers have the opportunity in Module 3 to listen to potential raw material from the real experiences with students, which can be used to develop the role playing in Module 4.

CHAPTER 8

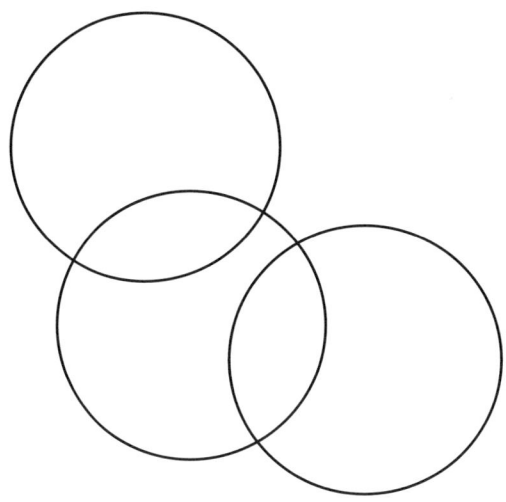

Module 3
Exploring Diversity in the Supervisory Relationship

Introduction and Round-Robin Responses

Welcome participants and invite them to share their responses to Reflecting Questions. Answering Reflecting Questions for Module 3 may provoke participants' anxiety and fears of exposure. They may be in denial of problems and have little to share because of avoidant behaviors. They may also be reluctant to share painful memories about past supervisory experiences or fear their stories may expose contradictions between stated principles and practices. For example, a participant may feel ashamed that she did not intervene with a supervisee whose religious beliefs precluded acceptance of a client's homosexual behavior. A participant may feel conflicted about how he talked to an Asian supervisee about the problems clients were having with her accent. Tell participants that Reflecting Questions for Module 3 are designed to increase awareness of discomfort in working with differences in supervision. This increased sense of unease actually represents growth and courage on the part of participants who can identify areas of discomfort. It is also a first step toward becoming more effective teachers for social work students.

Responses to Reflecting Questions serve as the stimulus for group discussions. If the Full 18-Hour Design is being used, extend the discussion as well as the mini lectures and exercise. If the Modified 14-Hour Design is being used, discussion time may be more limited. Also, use responses to Reflecting Questions as opportunities to explore real examples of avoidance, ambivalent attitudes toward exercising role power, and the management of boundary dilemmas. Avoidant behaviors typically include a lack of initiative or indirect communication in addressing differences and distancing relative to personal engagement with supervisees (Hendricks, 2003). Because being indirect is a preferred mode of communication in some cultures (such as Japanese), trainers must also assess if indirect communication is a reflection of the participant's culture or a strategy to avoid discomfort associated with addressing challenging diversity issues. Material generated from responses to Reflecting Questions becomes the catalyst for trainers to introduce new concepts, change perceptions, and establish new norms about how to manage cultural and social diversity issues in the supervisory relationship. If there is no discomfort about the questions, this peculiarity should be noted and reflected back to the group. Encourage sharing by describing your own struggles with addressing diversity issues with supervisees.

Mini Lecture Parallel Process

Objective
This lecture defines and explains the term "parallel process."

Instructions
Discuss parallel process by introducing the concept's basic principles.

Content
Parallel process refers to an unconscious process in which the issues and dynamics in one relationship are reenacted in another relationship; hence, the two relationships "parallel" each other. In reference to supervision, Doehrman (1976) has shown that what occurs (or doesn't occur) in the relationship between field instructor and student may be mirrored in the way that the student works with clients. It is also possible that the student will reenact in supervision what the student is experiencing with his or her client (Bogo, 1993). The implications related to teaching cultural competence in the field seem obvious. If field instructors avoid being direct in discussing physically visible or invisible differences between themselves and their students, such as age, gender, or ethnicity, students are more likely to avoid noticing or dealing with differences with their clients. Likewise, field instructors can assess dynamics in the student's relationship with the client by noting the dynamics that emerge in the supervisory relationship (Peterson, 1986). For example, if a Sudanese parent avoids addressing potentially volatile material

in the student-client relationship such as beating a child, which is a culturally sanctioned practice in Sudan but prohibited in the United States, the field instructor can assess this dynamic by noticing how the student circumvents issues about the case in discussions with the field instructor.

Mini Lecture Power

Objective

This lecture explores the multifaceted role of power in the supervisory relationship.

Instructions

Although the concept of power is core to the supervisory relationship (Kaiser, 1997; Peterson, 1992; Van Soest 2004), open discussion about the impact of the field instructor's role power or the power differential tends to be limited. Address the following areas related to power:

- Field instructors' discomfort with exercising their power
- Necessity to accept power
- Creative use of the power differential as a teaching tool

Content

Discuss the following issues of power as they relate to supervision.

Exploring Power Issues

Field instructors are reluctant to approach issues that create discomfort in the student (Marshack et al., 1994; Priddy, 2004). Field instructors may want to protect students from feeling badly about the mistakes they have made. They worry that discomfort will result in distancing, because the student will not feel safe. This concern is more likely when there are obvious cultural and social differences between the field instructor and student, for example, a young Caucasian supervisor and an older African American student. As a result, field instructors often wait for the student to initiate discussion of diversity issues under the misguided assumption that raising difficult topics could strain the relationship. This logic is highly problematic for a few reasons. Field instructors put their own needs for comfort and safety ahead of the student's learning. Field instructors abdicate responsibility by giving the student, who is in the more vulnerable position, the job of introducing topics that are likely to increase discomfort. In such cases, field instructors model avoidant behavior, which the student likely mimics with his or her clients.

MINI LECTURE Power

Instructions

Introduce the idea of accepting the inherent role of power as a field instructor. Explain how field instructors must use their power to initiate discussions about sensitive topics such as anger or privilege, help students tolerate and manage their own discomfort, and model the appropriate use of authority. Then continue this part of the lecture by discussing the following ideas.

Accepting Power

Power is also central to diversity issues (Pinderhughes, 1989). Differences in social class, for example, often reflect differences in social status. Differences in sexual orientation or gender identity may reflect oppressive judgments by people who deem themselves to be more moral or superior. These power dynamics play alongside the power differential that defines the supervisory relationship. To the degree that field instructors inappropriately minimize the power inherent in their role, they also may minimize the need to address power differences created by social disparities. If field instructors come to terms with their power in the supervisory relationship, they are less likely to be avoidant in addressing the role inequities between themselves and their students, as well as the social inequities between either themselves and their students or students and their clients. Field instructors' willingness to come to terms with their power is a critical first step in addressing cultural and social diversity issues with students.

Instructions

Address how the power differential or difference in status between field instructor and student creates real-life opportunities to explore power-related issues, such as the privilege of holding authority over those with less power and the potential to use power oppressively. Also discuss how these particular dynamics contribute to discriminatory behavior in relationships and situations where there are social inequities. Examples of relationships with unearned privilege might include relationships where there are differences in race, gender identity, economics, sexual orientation, physical and mental disabilities, religion, and so on.

Continue the lecture with the following points.

Using the Power Differential as a Teaching Tool

Within the supervisory relationship, there is opportunity to explore these dynamics for learning, because the student may experience feelings of injustice if he or she perceives the field instructor's exercise of power as unfairly controlling of the student's behavior. For example, if a student receives a poor evaluation or is denied opportunities because the field instructor decides he or she is not sufficiently prepared, the student may feel unduly criticized or picked on. These feelings of injustice highlight the reality and significance of the power differential in the supervisory relationship and can mimic the discrimination clients may have experienced, albeit in a more diluted form.

Like their clients, students may be reluctant to voice their concerns because they fear retribution or perceive themselves as powerless over the consequences. When the field instructor initiates a discussion about the perceived injustice and demonstrates how such a topic can be handled productively, it can provide an important learning experience about how to address inequities. It may, for example, give students the chance to be forthcoming with their frustrations and concerns without negative ramifications. Moreover, if a field instructor engages students in a dialogue about their reactions to the field instructor, including their experiences of the power differential in supervision, it is easier to take the next step toward discussing how these issues of power, privilege, and oppression influence students' relationships with clients. The supervisory relationship, therefore, offers a laboratory in the present to face intense feelings, process interactions around sensitive issues, and internalize the growth-enhancing effects of having learned to navigate emotionally loaded topics (Van Soest, 2004). These experiences also give students more confidence to take risks in the future and explore anxiety-provoking subjects with clients that highlight social inequities or differences between them.

Mini Lecture **Boundaries**

Objective

This lecture explores how to create effective and safe boundaries in the field instructor/student relationship.

Instructions

Discuss the following ideas related to boundaries and supervision.

Content

Field instructors avoid diversity issues because they fear that being direct and personal will be disrespectful of a student's boundaries. Moreover, field instructors who are ambivalent about their power often have trouble knowing where and how to draw boundaries based on context (Peterson, 1992). Uncertainty and worry about possible repercussions keep field instructors away from issues of cultural and social diversity. Therefore, field instructors establish the norm that avoidance, rather than the willingness to draw appropriate boundaries, creates the illusion of safety in the agency work environment.

MINI LECTURE Boundaries

Field instructors need to be explicit about establishing boundaries for safety. If a student makes racist comments, the field instructor needs to confront the behavior because it threatens the safety necessary for a productive supervisory relationship and, by extension, the safety of clients. If a school of social work places students with limited English in a practice setting that requires greater language facility, the field instructor needs to draw limits by discussing with the school representative the additional problems the situation creates for clients, the student, and the agency, as well as the possible need for a different arrangement. If a young Asian American female student is reluctant to share with an older Caucasian male field instructor, the field instructor needs to increase safety by actively exploring possible reasons, including the student's cultural norms, concerns about evaluation, worries about saving face because of the field instructor's judgment, negative history with males, and the student's need for support to engage in meaningful self-examination. These examples demonstrate how boundaries are created when field instructors take positions and are direct and personal in addressing differences related to diversity issues with students. Moreover, the ability to set limits and take stands is one of the skills students must have to challenge effectively and combat racist attitudes and oppressive behaviors. When the field instructor models these boundary-setting behaviors, students are more likely to internalize the experience and draw on it in the future.

Give the following suggestions to participants to increase safety:

1. From the beginning, discuss students' expectations for educational supervision. Expectations include discussing cultural and social differences in the supervisory relationship and differences between the students and clients as they relate to the purpose of the agency's work.

2. Clarify differences between therapy and supervision. Students should be told explicitly that they are expected to increase their self-awareness by using supervision for reflection and self-examination *related to their work with clients*. Moreover, students should expect personal engagement with field instructors around vital issues specific to clients.

3. Be willing to form a learning partnership by owning mistakes and struggles with students. Issues may be drawn from the field instructor's history or may emerge from the current supervisory relationship. This modeling makes it easier for students to admit their own errors, confusion, or insecurities. Moreover, when the student sees the field instructor confronting anxiety in order to be direct in addressing differences, the student is supported to behave in a similar manner with clients.

4. Present the idea of cultural competence as a continuum of development, that is, there are no graduates (NASW, 2001). Everyone is a work in

progress, including the field instructor. The expectation is that both supervisor and student are willing to struggle and endure the discomfort that accompanies the decision to address issues of cultural and social diversity and disparities.

5. Help students understand the positives in having a "beginner's mind." When they accept that they do not have answers, they are freer to meet the client without preconceived ideas or agendas. Moreover, they may be better able to hear their clients as their clients hope to be heard.

Exercise Exploring Dilemmas

Objective

The purpose of this exercise is for participants to share difficult experiences in the safety of a small group.

Instructions

Lead the group in the following steps:

1. Separate into small groups (3 to 5 people).
2. List differences between yourselves and your students or between your students and their clients. Describe the experiences you have had in addressing these differences with students. Describe the dilemmas/challenges and how you handled them.
3. What specific assignments, readings, or cultural events have you provided to students in order to increase cultural competence, for example, seeing the film, *The Laramie Project*, which is a true story of the murder of Matthew Shepherd, a young gay man from Laramie, Wyoming. In the future, what materials could you use to increase this awareness? What untapped resources could be used?

Processing

Ask participants to report back to the group and describe their positive experiences. As participants describe dilemmas, listen for and comment on the following themes:
- Impotence
- Fear of consequences
- Anger and frustration

EXERCISE Exploring Dilemmas

- Lack of boundaries
- Possible parallel processes for students and their clients

Also, solicit group problem solving as well. Generate a list of ideas for increasing cultural competence and write them down on poster pads. Comment on the creativity and sound ideas that are shared. This exercise can be used at any time during Module 3. It generates information that can be used as the basis for mini lectures and underscores important points made in the mini lectures if given earlier during the training.

Conclusion

Ask participants to reflect on what they experienced in the session specific to their work with students. Pose the following questions to the participants:

1. What experiences in this session were the most and least valuable to you in your role as field instructor?
2. What ideas did you gain that could enhance how you deal with diversity issues with students?
3. Did you notice any points of anxiety or discomfort in today's group? What did you decide to do with those feelings and why? What, if anything, does that suggest to you about what students may experience? What are the implications for you?
4. What else do you need to become more effective in teaching cultural competence?

Since Module 3 challenges perceptions, participants are apt to feel stimulated, challenged, uncomfortable, and ambivalent about the future direction of the training. They may recognize that they tend to be reactive to differences and to addressing issues related to cultural and social diversity rather than being in charge. They also realize that they need to take risks in relationships with students by being more direct and personally engaged. Assure participants that Module 4 will provide skill development related to addressing social inequities and diversity issues with students. Also, encourage participants to respect and tolerate the disequilibrium that accompanies change, which may be their experience at the end of Module 3. Distribute Reflecting Questions.

Reflecting Questions:
Effecting Change in the Supervisory Relationship

1. Think of a time in your personal or professional life when you took a risk to share or do something that was important to you even though you had no idea what the results might be. Consider the internal process that you experienced in trying to reach the decision to take the risk. What happened that finally enabled you to do so?

2. List several more examples in supervision that you now recognize as times when you avoided discussing an issue that could have been an opportunity to promote or enhance cultural competence. What do you now understand contributed to these blind spots in behavior? How would you act differently now?

3. In the past, we thought the goal of cultural competence was to be color-blind, that is, to emphasize sameness rather than celebrate diversity. How is it possible to appreciate our common human experience in the context of honoring differences? What are the implications for supervision?

CHAPTER 9

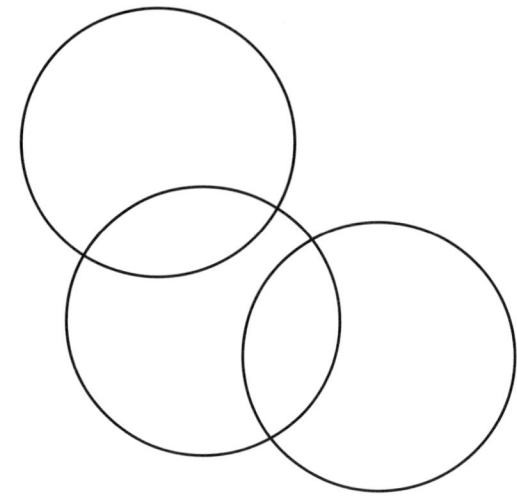

Module 4
Effecting Change in the Supervisory Relationship

Introduction

Before Module 4, use all information from previous sessions to construct role playing tailored to the unique characteristics of the individual participants. Participants are assigned to pairs as "field instructor" and "student." Construct role playing for each dyad and focus on real interpersonal differences. Each person is given a brief fact situation that helps structure the interaction. Specifically, those who play students present their field instructors with client dilemmas that have made them uncomfortable and hesitant. The dilemmas also cause field instructors to retreat because the vignettes purposefully highlight their own personal issues or target real disparities in the role-playing dyads. The purpose of the role playing is to help participants experience the directness, honesty, and quality of connection necessary for exploring diversity in supervision.

Find examples of role playing in appendix C. Note: During the exercise, each participant is given a slip of paper with a brief description of his or her part in the role playing. Participants are asked *not to share* the information on their slip of paper with their partner.

EXERCISE 1 Role Playing

Round-Robin Responses

Welcome participants and invite them to share their responses to Reflecting Questions. Questions 1 and 2 evoke stories about the consequences of risking new behaviors. Question 3 elicits the emerging development of new principles for addressing diversity issues. Acknowledge and show deep respect for participants' struggles, insights, and awareness of avoidant behaviors. Emphasize the importance of staying "in the process" rather than being a finished product. Mention the significance of sharing a similar journey despite our differences. Value participants by referencing their comments or stories and using them as examples for illustrating concepts, such as risk taking, tolerating discomfort, or observing the parallel process with students.

Introduce the skill-building laboratory for Module 4. The goal of this laboratory is to help participants learn to use the supervisory relationship as a medium for addressing cultural and social differences and disparities in the client-worker relationship and experience the use of directness to foster growth. Outline the procedure and answer questions. The procedure contains five parts:

- Role-playing dyads
- Group consultation
- Reconvened role playing
- Exercise processing
- Didactic handout

Exercise 1 Role Playing

Objective

The purpose of this exercise is to delineate issues that hinder the exploration of diversity in the supervisory relationship. Until student workers have examined their issues concerning social and cultural diversity, it is not possible to assist clients who may need to examine similar issues (Pinderhughes, 1989).

Instructions

Lead participants in the following steps:

1. Each of you has been designated as either "field instructor" or "student."
2. You will be paired by trainers and given a brief script to follow. Please *do not* share the scripts with each other.

EXERCISE 2 Group Consultation

3. All of you will be role playing simultaneously. No one will observe except the trainers who are gathering information to be used later in the session.
4. After 15 minutes the role playing will be interrupted. "Field instructors" will meet in a group to review their experiences and receive additional guidance from the trainers. "Students" will meet in a different group to review their experiences as students. Please give yourselves as much physical space as possible to reduce interference from conversations in other dyads.

During this exercise, rotate between dyads as unobtrusively as possible. Collect information on the following:
- Tenor of the interaction
- Student needs to address with clients
- Avoidant behavior of the field instructor in dealing with the student

Exercise 2 Group Consultation

Objective
The purpose of this exercise is to delineate barriers to addressing diversity issues in the supervisory relationship and provide suggestions for handling them.

Instructions
Interrupt the role playing after about 15 minutes. For this exercise, one or two trainers facilitate the group for field instructors, and another one facilitates the group for students.

Group for Field Instructors

1. Use a round-robin format to briefly review each case and ask participants the following questions:
   a. What are the diversity issues with the client?
   b. What are you doing to help the student with those issues?
   c. How is the student responding to you?
   d. Are there parallels between the student and client and you and the student?
   e. Does the student's response to you mirror the client's response to the student? If so, how?

f. Do your reactions to the student mirror the student's reactions to the client? If so, how?
2. Provide participants with feedback focused on the parallel process and how the field instructor can address what needs to happen between student and client by explicitly focusing on the interaction between the student and the field instructor.
3. Offer guidance on how to address students more directly and personally relative to the supervisory relationship and/or the student's interaction with the client(s). (Use the "Being Direct in Supervision" handout in appendix B as a resource.)

Group for Students
1. Use a round-robin format to review briefly each student's experience with the field instructor and ask students to identify manifestations of their own avoidance and the impact of the field instructor on their ability to be forthcoming.
2. Ask the participants the following questions:
    a. What is happening between you and the client?
    b. What diversity issues are you avoiding?
    c. What are you doing in supervision to distance from those issues?
    d. What is the tenor of the interaction between you and your field instructor?
    e. What could your field instructor have done to make it easier for you to discuss differences?

Exercise 3 **Reconvened Role Playing**

Objective
The purpose of this exercise is for the participants who are field instructors to implement ideas gained from the group consultation.

Instructions
Lead the group through these steps:
1. Reconvene the supervisory dyads and continue role playing for another 15 minutes.

MINI LECTURE Didactic Handout

2. Test out new knowledge with students. Trainers will circulate among you to provide help and observe changes as a result of the consultation.

Processing

Ask for volunteers to share information about the skills they learned during the exercises. Make statements throughout to help participants apply comments about the role playing or new knowledge to abstract principles, such as parallel process, the power differential, boundary setting, role power, and being direct and personal. During this time, ask the following questions:

1. What did you initially experience in your role as either field instructor or student? What issues related to social and cultural diversity were being avoided? What behaviors did students use to avoid the issues with clients? What behaviors did field instructors use to avoid the issues with students?

2. How did the behavior of the field instructors change as a result of the group consultation? How did you feel about bringing the new knowledge back to supervision? What helped you to move beyond your own personal discomfort? What did you do differently with your student? How did your student respond? Describe the sense of risk you experienced during the exercise.

3. How did the supervisory relationship change for the student after field instructors received consultation? How did you respond to this change? How do you think you might behave with clients as a result of the postconsultation supervision?

Mini Lecture **Didactic Handout**

Objective

This lecture identifies effective steps in being direct with students.

Instructions

Give participants the handout, "Being Direct in Supervision." (See appendix B.) The handout includes a specific protocol for addressing issues about diversity with students. It identifies common fears that prohibit candidness and authenticity in supervision and details the steps of the process that participants have just experienced. The handout also illustrates how to transfer this experiential learning from the supervision to students' work with clients. The trainer uses examples from the role-playing laboratory as illustrations as well. After the handout is explained, participants discuss how they might use the handout in their work with supervisees. Participants are cautioned to be sensitive to cultural differences relative to directness. The steps in reviewing the protocol are the following:

1. Introduction of client situation related to social and cultural diversity
2. Expression of concern about student's behavior
3. Student's reaction to the concern
4. Exploration of behavior and its probable impact on clients
5. Options for different behavior
6. Addressing the student's fear
7. Results from implementing different behavior

Use the pronoun "you" or "we" depending on the tone you prefer to emphasize.

Content

The experience you had in being direct and personal in the role-playing laboratory can be broken down into stages. The stages are outlined in a protocol that is described in the handout, "Being Direct in Supervision" in appendix B.

Introduction of Client Situation Related to Social and Cultural Diversity

Because the field instructor does not want to get ahead of the student, it is best to wait until a topic related to social or cultural diversity introduces itself into supervision. The field instructor may have some clues about important material related to social and cultural diversity that should be addressed with the student. However, it is better to wait to introduce topics or concerns until an incident arises that is naturally related to a client or work situation. Moreover, when the field instructor can associate the topic with a specific client or work-related issue, the rationale for why the field instructor is bringing up the topic will be clearer to the student.

The first clue the field instructor has about the topic often will come from his or her reaction to the student's behavior. The field instructor can ask himself or herself the following question: "What does the supervisee's behavior tell me about the supervisee?" For example, if the student is talking about an evacuee from Hurricane Katrina but does not mention race, the field instructor might ponder what that behavior tells her or him about the student. The answers will give the field instructor hypotheses to explore the student's attitudes, history, or behaviors with this client and other clients.

Expression of Concern About Student's Behavior

The field instructor begins the exploration by *first* describing his or her own feelings and fears about introducing the topic. This self-disclosure helps solicit the

MINI LECTURE Didactic Handout

student's engagement at a personal level. Moreover, it reminds the student that the field instructor cares about the student, that the supervisory relationship is important to the field instructor, and that the field instructor is taking a risk by approaching a sensitive topic. Next the field instructor describes the student's behavior and his or her concern. For example, "I am concerned about your tendency not to identify the race or ethnicity of the clients you talk about in supervision."

Student's Reaction to the Concern

Before going into the topic, the field instructor asks the student to share his or her feelings about the topic raised by the field instructor. The field instructor also asks the student how the student feels toward the instructor. These requests and the student's responses help the field instructor and student stay connected and reduce the possibility that the student's energy will be spent trying to manage or contain strong reactions to the topic raised rather than being able to move ahead in the exploration with the field instructor. The requests also model for the student that affectively charged responses are permitted and necessary to the work. Finally, the field instructor's questions lay the groundwork for the risk taking necessary to exploring sensitive or taboo topics.

Exploration of Behavior and its Probable Impact on Clients

The field instructor asks the student what the student knows about the topic. This question lets the field instructor know whether the topic is new or familiar. Prior to exploring the topic in relation to clients or the work environment, the field instructor also broadens the area to be explored by asking the student for his or her thoughts about the topic generally. For example, "Have other people like your teachers or previous supervisors talked to you about the tendency not to delineate important social or cultural characteristics about clients? What do you think this is all about really for you? How would you identify the social and cultural differences between us? Which ones are hardest to name?" This exploration furthers the field instructor's understanding of the size and significance of the topic and gauges the student's reluctance to engage with the field instructor in a deeper examination.

After the field instructor has information about the student relative to the topic, the field instructor explores the topic relative to its impact on clients. The intent of the exploration is both to examine and suggest that the student's behavior is having an impact on the client and the student's relationship with the client. For example, "If you have trouble identifying significant and visible social and cultural characteristics and the differences between you and the client, how do you think your discomfort with these obvious differences might be playing out in your relationship with your client? If you were to recognize those differences verbally in talking with the client, how do you think the client would feel?" The field instructor also explores the student's beliefs that might contribute to the topic. For example, the student might be fearful that initiating a discussion about an obvious issue might be misinterpreted or might offend the client. The field instructor examines the reality of the fears and discusses what the student can do about his or her concerns. "Do you think you could ask the client, like I did with you earlier, about what the client is feeling or thinking about you or the topic you raised? Then you wouldn't have to guess."

Options for Different Behavior

The field instructor discusses options for new behavior in relationship to the topic. The field instructor engages the student in generating a variety of ideas about what the student could do differently. Usually this discussion creates a number of possibilities and concomitant fears in the student as he or she mentally rehearses the possible consequences. The field instructor elicits those fears by asking things like, "What are you worried might happen?" "What's the worst thing that could happen? What do you think will happen between us because of our talking about some of our differences?"

Addressing the Student's Fear

The field instructor addresses the student's concerns by evaluating the likelihood of negative fallout. Their mutual examination might result in further discussion about options, modifications, or tips on how to reduce feared consequences. The field instructor may suggest role playing so the student can test his or her concerns or gain ideas from the field instructor in the context of the role playing about alternative responses.

Results From Implementing Different Behavior

The field instructor gets feedback after the student has had a chance to implement new behavior. The feedback lets the field instructor know if he or she needs to do still more with the student. The feedback also furnishes the field instructor with the opportunity to meaningfully relate the student's experience to theory and/or social work values. The field instructor may broaden the learning by transferring the new behavior to the student's other clients or work-related situations, which deepens the student's understanding of theory.

Direct communication will likely advance rather than harm the teaching/learning relationship between field instructor and student. Moreover, attention to the indirect communication often associated with avoidance will result

MINI LECTURE Didactic Handout

in greater strides in cultural competence for the supervisee. However, the strategy to be used with supervisees varies and derives from an assessment of each person's learning needs, learning styles, cultural context, and communication patterns. The strategy also varies based on the cultural context of the field instructor. In some cultures, for example, direct communication is offensive. Indirect communication, therefore, may reflect a culture's mores in addition to or instead of a person's individual discomfort with diversity issues. Consequently, the strategy relative to directness may vary based on the cultural context of the field instructor, the field instructor's assessment of the student, and the degree of directness that is appropriate in a particular situation. The goal, however, is for the field instructor to be proficient in using both direct and indirect methods to effect change and to be intentional in his or her efforts to reduce the barriers to examining diversity issues in supervision by using the supervisory relationship to address sensitive areas.

It is also important to clarify that being personal refers to the freedom to comment on the interaction in the supervisory relationship and explore responses to sensitive areas that might otherwise be considered private, for example, experiences of discrimination that the student has experienced and so on. The decision by the field instructor to engage more personally must be thoughtful, intentional, and directly relevant to client-related material.

Conclusion

Ask participants to reflect on the group and select key moments of learning. In response to comments, make the following points:

1. Directness paradoxically increases safety and vulnerability within a relationship.
2. Risk taking is the other side of avoidance.
3. The agony of being direct is countered by the pride of no longer avoiding what is in the middle of the room.

Finishing Module 4 concludes the focus on the Relationship With the Student Supervisee. The diversity training focus changes to the Relationship With the Agency. The Reflecting Questions illustrate this shift and are used to help participants make the transition to Module 5.

Reflecting Questions: Diversity and Your Agency

1. How would you describe the general culture and management style of your agency? How do they support or inhibit agency cultural competence?

2. What aspect of your agency is most culturally competent and why? What would you suggest is the most immediate need in developing cultural competence in your agency?

3. What have you done at your agency to make it more receptive to diversity issues or to increase its cultural competence?

4. Think about a time when your agency struggled with the issue of cultural competence relative to privilege and oppression, for example, racism, sexism, and so on. How was the issue handled by the agency in terms of its public face, and how was it handled internally with the staff?

5. How are privilege and oppression manifested in your agency?

PART 4

Relationship With Agency

Focus: The focus of these modules is on challenging disempowering beliefs that impede movement toward social change.

Objectives:

1. Increase awareness of disempowering beliefs
2. Challenge the impact of past experiences on current behavior
3. Increase field instructor's confidence and energy to intervene significantly at the agency level

Module 5:   Diversity and Your Agency
            Introduction and Round-Robin Responses
            Mini Lecture: Cultural Competence Continuum
            Exercise: Agency Assessment
            Conclusion
            Reflecting Questions: Future Action
Module 6:   Future Action
            Introduction
            Round-Robin Responses
            Mini Lecture: Disempowerment
            Exercise: Roots of Disempowerment
            Mini Lecture: Changing Perspectives: The Agency as Your Client
            Conclusion

Module 5 is used to help participants assess the multicultural competence of their agency, identify areas of strength and weakness within the agency, and recognize the roles participants have or have not played in helping the agency to become more culturally and socially diverse and culturally competent. Participants will likely feel stuck, frustrated, and overwhelmed after they acknowledge the agency's problems and the role they have played in advocating or inhibiting action toward change. These feelings result in avoidant behaviors. Module 6 is used to identify disempowering beliefs and their origins, and provides tools to intervene in enduring attitudes that prevent participants from becoming agents of social change or helping their agencies become more culturally competent. Module 6 (Future Action) is also used to conclude the training and has participants make contracts with themselves about their future behavior related to diversity.

CHAPTER 10

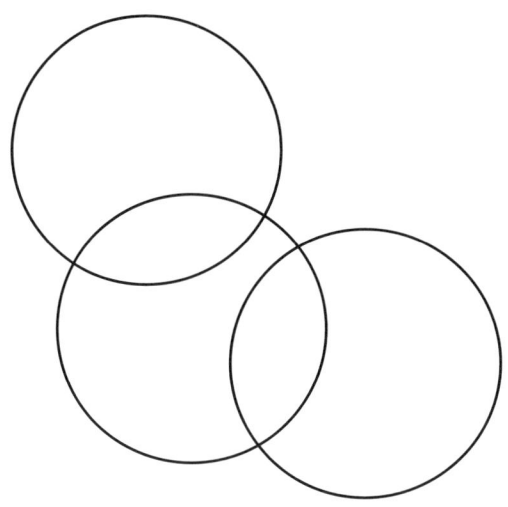

Module 5
Diversity and Your Agency

Introduction and Round-Robin Responses

A warm welcome is given to the group. Initiate the round-robin review of Reflecting Questions. Since the questions ask participants to discuss their agencies, remind participants of the confidentiality agreement and provide support for participants' increased sense of vulnerability.

Mini Lecture Cultural Competence Continuum

Objective

The purpose of this mini lecture is to present the six distinct points of the Cultural Competence Continuum.

Content

The Cultural Competence Continuum was developed by Cross, Bazron, Dennis, and Isaacs (1989). Cultural competence is defined as "a set of congruent behaviors, attitudes, and policies that come together in a system, agency, or among professionals and enable that system, agency, or those professionals to work effectively in cross-cultural situations" (p. iv). The continuum defines six items beginning from the negative endpoint of cultural destructiveness and moving toward the positive endpoint of cultural proficiency. The six points on the continuum are the following:

MINI LECTURE Cultural Competence Continuum

1. Cultural Destructiveness
2. Cultural Incapacity
3. Cultural Blindness
4. Cultural Pre-competence
5. Cultural Competence
6. Cultural Proficiency (see appendix F for handouts)

Review each of the points below in detail with the participants.

Cultural Destructiveness

The attitudes of agency personnel and the policies and practices of the agency itself are destructive and extremely oppressive to cultures and individuals within the culture. Extreme examples of cultural destructiveness are programs, agencies, or institutions that actively participate in genocide or in seriously damaging cultures. Examples include the U.S. Exclusion Laws of 1885–1965 that prohibited Asians from bringing spouses into the country, and the policy of the U.S. government to remove Native American children from reservations and place them in boarding schools.

Cultural Incapacity

Agencies and systems do not seek to be culturally destructive or oppressive, but lack the capacity to help minority clients or communities. Agencies remain extremely biased and their predominant belief is in the racial superiority of the dominant group. Agency staff, policies, and practices are paternalistic toward the "lesser" group, and resources are usually channeled away from the lesser groups in favor of the dominant groups. Hiring practices are discriminatory, and there are subtle messages that people belonging to the lesser group are not welcome or valued. Examples of this are school segregation and the philosophy of "separate but equal."

Cultural Blindness

Agencies believe that they are unbiased because they treat everyone the same. Agencies maintain that traditional approaches that work with the dominant culture are universally applicable. This frame of reference is based on privilege. Being in the position of privilege allows one to have no awareness that the dominant culture is inherently tied to power and that this power will be experienced by other groups as "power over." The thinking of "We're all the same" is a part of the privilege for the dominant group. Agency staff, policies, and practices ignore

MINI LECTURE Cultural Competence Continuum

cultural strengths of other groups and, in fact, encourage assimilation. Outcomes are measured by how closely clients match the dominant pattern. Examples of this are special projects that target minorities that are funded only if money is available and with very little input from the targeted community.

Cultural Pre-Competence

Agencies exhibit a heightened awareness of power and privilege and movement in a positive direction. They realize their weaknesses in serving underrepresented groups and make attempts to improve. Agencies might experiment by hiring minority staff or explore how to reach people from underrepresented groups in their service area. Agency staff, policies, and practices begin to seek new ways to reach underrepresented groups more successfully. The caution here is that it is easy to believe that accomplishing one small step or activity fulfills the obligation to the underrepresented group. An example here is tokenism.

Cultural Competence

Agencies are characterized by acceptance and respect for difference. At this point, agencies will engage in a continuing self-assessment regarding culture and will seek advice and consultation from minority communities. Policies and practices of the agency are adapted to better meet the needs of underrepresented groups. Agencies clearly view minority groups as distinctly different from one another and acknowledge the differences within groups.

Cultural Proficiency

Differences are held in high esteem. There is a considerable awareness of the dynamics of power, difference, and privilege among all members of the agency. The agency seeks to add to the knowledge base by conducting research, developing new approaches, and publishing and disseminating results of research projects. Also, agency staff, policies, and practices promote empowerment of underrepresented groups and actively advocate on their behalf. Specialists in culturally competent practice are hired on staff.

Instructions

Continue the mini lecture by noting how the Cultural Competence Continuum is helpful in several ways. It gives a standard by which to measure the agencies where we work. It gives an indication of strengths and areas for improvement. Ask participants to consider an assessment of their agencies by thinking about the following components, which are derived, in part, from the 10-S framework of organizational effectivness for nonprofit organizations developed by Bailey and Aronoff (2004).

MINI LECTURE Cultural Competence Continuum

Content

- *Demographics*: Where is your agency located? What are the demographics of the surrounding area? Is it accessible from all surrounding communities and to all potential stakeholders?

- *Knowledge of the underrepresented communities*: What does the agency staff know of the history and experiences of the underrepresented communities?

- *Interaction with people from the underrepresented communities*: What groups are represented on your agency's board of directors? How does your agency get input from stakeholders and underrepresented groups to assist in program development?

- *Agency practice, policy, and procedure*: Does the mission statement explicitly include a reference to multicultural competency? How do the bylaws and strategic plan reflect cultural competence?

- *Agency printed materials*: How do the agency brochures, annual reports, outreach materials, intake forms, and so forth reflect cultural competence?

- *Agency facilities*: What allowances do your agency's facilities make for people with disabilities?

- *Composition of staff, volunteers, and board members*: What is the diversity among your agency's personnel? Does the diversity reflect the population served by your agency?

- *Staff personnel assessment that includes cultural competency*: How does your agency ensure that the staff has skills to work with diverse populations? Do annual reviews include the measurement of goals related to increasing the staff's cultural competence?

- *Training opportunities*: Are these available on an ongoing basis? Are there formal and informal opportunities for staff to share their skills and learn from each other? Are opportunities provided for staff to enhance their multicultural competence?

- *Service delivery issues*: Does your agency stay open in the evening and on weekends?

- *Advocacy*: How does your agency support change on a policy level?

- *Organizational culture*: How does your agency attend to possible dysfunction in the organizational culture? How open is your agency to restructuring its organization, if necessary, to improve the workplace environment? Are systems in place to help mediate should cultural differences become a source of friction in the workplace?

Exercise Agency Assessment

Objective
The purpose of this exercise is to use the Cultural Competence Continuum to identify the elements in the participants' agencies that support efforts to become multiculturally competent and the elements that detract from this goal.

Instructions
Lead the group through the following steps:

1. Break into dyads.
2. Take turns talking with each other about the other person's agency. Closely examine your agency by using the Worksheet: Assessing the Cultural Competency of the Agency. (See appendix D.) Your partner is to listen without interruption or distraction. Your partner can ask questions to clarify what you are reporting.
3. When you have finished, rank your agency along the Cultural Competence Continuum on the second page of the worksheet.
4. Your partner will follow the same procedure to evaluate his or her agency.

Processing
Participants share their thoughts and feelings using a round-robin format. Write down their responses on easel-pad sheets or flip-chart paper. This visual image will help to identify emerging themes. Acknowledge that it is normal for participants to feel discomfort or ambivalence in scrutinizing their agencies. To process the exercise, use the following questions to focus the discussion among the group members:

1. To your knowledge, what attempts have been made by your agency to become multiculturally competent? With what specific outcomes?
2. What are the major supports and obstacles to developing multicultural competence in your agency and/or community?
3. What do you see as the most logical next steps for your agency to become more multiculturally competent?
4. What are the most positive practices or attempts by the agency to become more multiculturally competent?
5. What did you learn about your agency? How do you feel about what you learned?

EXERCISE Agency Assessment

6. What was this exercise like for you?
7. Realistically speaking, what can you personally commit to doing to help your agency become more multiculturally competent?

When participants are finished, identify common themes and begin to articulate the collective mindset.

Participants are apt to share reactions that underscore frustrations with their agencies as well as feelings of disempowerment and helplessness. "Other staff at my agency use the Latino/Latina social workers as translators." "We service a rural community that is homophobic but the agency director keeps hiring only gay or lesbian staff." Moreover, because participants have just assessed their agencies, they may have also reawakened memories of past efforts to evoke change or be more sensitive to how far the agency has yet to go. They may state that they feel extremely overwhelmed at the thought of working to improve the agency's competency. The challenge may appear to be all consuming and impossible to shift. "It's just tokenism in my agency. We have one of each." "The agency won't even give us time off from work to attend trainings like this." This discussion gives participants a basis for comparison and reflection about the multicultural competency of their individual agencies. It also gives you the content for Module 6, which focuses on feelings of disempowerment as a basis for avoidant behavior.

Conclusion

Ask participants for their overall reactions to the mini lecture and worksheet assessment. Participants may indicate worry over having exposed their agencies' weaknesses, frustration over feeling historically blocked by their agencies when they tried to make changes, and/or ambivalent about what remains to be done. Reassure participants that the discomfort they are feeling is normal and that it was intentionally provoked as a prelude to Module 6, which is designed to give them tools for taking positive action.

Distribute the last set of Reflecting Questions to participants. Explain that because these Reflecting Questions are the last ones in the training, you are asking them to evaluate all of their learning. Also give them the handouts in appendix F. Inform participants that some time will be allotted in the following session to provide verbal feedback about the training. Thank participants for their contributions.

Reflecting Questions: Future Action

1. What idea or skill do you know you will take with you to enhance your practice and/or future supervisory relationships with students?
2. Briefly discuss how you think these discoveries will contribute to your effectiveness as a field instructor.
3. What realistic commitments can you make to continue your growth as a culturally competent practitioner and teacher?
4. What realistic commitment can you make to attempt to make your agency more culturally competent?
5. What did you delight in and what did you find most disturbing or uncomfortable during the training?
6. Identify one or two highlights or "aha" moments in your experience with the training.
7. How did you experience the group process? What effect did the number of facilitators and the size of the group have on you?
8. Please give specific suggestions for ways we can improve future trainings.

Questions 1–4 are considered essential.

CHAPTER 11

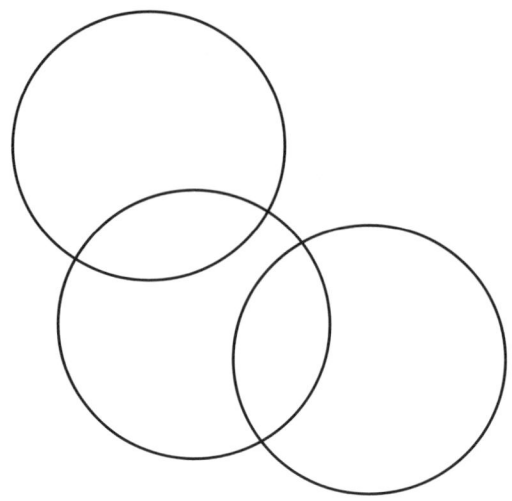

Module 6
Future Action

Introduction

The purpose of this module is to increase the field instructor's effectiveness as a staff member to intervene with social disparities, prejudicial statements or behaviors, racism, or other forms of oppression that could help the agency become more multiculturally competent. Effectiveness is increased by participants becoming more aware of disempowering beliefs that impede their actions and by altering the perception of the agency's omnipotence by reconceptualizing the agency as a client.

Round-Robin Responses

Welcome the group. Initiate the round-robin review of Reflecting Questions. Guide the discussion and present the following questions:

- What are the negative (disempowering) messages that you hear from yourself—or negative self-talk—that preclude being effective?
- What are your reactions to problems that you are aware of in your agency?
- How do you see yourself in relation to these problems?

Watch for participants' frustrations about the vast complexity of problems in their agencies. Examples of answers to above questions could include the following:

- "I don't want to rock the boat."

- "Why do I have to be the one to educate everybody else?" (This answer might be the response of a participant of color.)
- "I'm not ready, as a man, to support women leaders."

These answers reflect the common theme of removing or distancing oneself from being responsible to promote change or disqualifying oneself from taking action to remedy the situation. Highlight this theme by noting the similarities in participants' responses. When you the trainer articulate the feeling of disempowerment and distancing, the group is able to step back and reflect on the common theme of disempowerment.

Mini Lecture **Disempowerment**

Objective

The purpose of this mini lecture is to examine oppression and disempowering experiences that occurred early in life and to explore the conclusions participants drew about themselves as a result.

Instructions

Lead the group through the following lecture about disempowerment.

Content

Often our present-day actions are rooted in early experiences that taught us how to manage life's situations. Hence, the lessons we bring into adulthood are based on experiences we had as children or teenagers. These lessons may have served us in our early life, but often they are outdated and no longer useful to us as adults when we are in positions of influence and can make choices.

In the early modules, we recognized the various social identities that each of us has and celebrated the differences by telling personal stories about traditions we experienced in our families of origin. Also, in the exercise, titled Internalized Attitudes, in Module 1, we acknowledged that we have internalized negative attitudes about the groups we belong to. These internalized negative attitudes are the result of oppression in our society. For example, if we select one of our social identities—gender—then we can begin to think of the various negative attitudes that we have acquired as a result of oppression and sexism. For women, these negative messages may be about being "dumb," "weak," "emotionally unstable," and so on. For men, these negative messages may be about being "sexually promiscuous," "stupid," "emotionally numb," and so forth. For people who are gay, lesbian, bisexual, or transgendered, the oppression of heterosexism is mixed with the sexism

EXERCISE Roots of Disempowerment

they experience. For people who are poor, negative messages may revolve around stereotypes, such as "trailer trash," "having out-of-wedlock babies," "being a welfare mother," or "being a drain on the country's resources." When we consider *all* of our social identities and the groups to which we belong, it becomes clear that as we live each day, we are bombarded by messages that are disempowering.

Often, in very subtle and powerful ways, the disempowering experiences of oppression that occur early in our lives and their resulting beliefs leave us with feelings of powerlessness and frustration. Even though these experiences happened early in life, we carry the beliefs with us every day and depend on these beliefs to help us manage present challenges. One of the manifestations of having internalized these negative attitudes is self-doubt and incapacity. Being in the subordinate position may lead you to doubt your view of reality because it is not affirmed by your work environment. It may lead you to hesitate to speak up when a genuine need is recognized, perhaps thinking, "Who am I to raise this concern?" or "What right do I have to say this is wrong?"

When confronted by the problems of achieving multicultural competence in the agency, we are likely to revert to these beliefs and repeat the avoidant behaviors that interfere with progress toward cultural proficiency. These beliefs that many of us carry may be part of what we avoid, that is, the elephant in the room. Admitting that we have feelings of discomfort, frustration, and disempowerment makes us feel vulnerable and small. In order to be effective agents of social change within our work environments, we must name the elephant (the discomfort), reevaluate its impact on our present-day behavior, and develop successful attitudes and skills for undertaking the challenge of promoting organizational growth, combating racism and other "isms," and pursuing cultural competence.

Exercise Roots of Disempowerment

Objective

The purpose of this exercise is to examine disempowering experiences that occurred early in life and challenge the conclusions participants drew about themselves as a result.

Instructions

The aforementioned conclusions are referred to as "beliefs" to suggest that they are changeable. Ask participants to reflect on how these beliefs from the past control their present-day responses to diversity issues in their agencies. An important ingredient in the effectiveness of this exercise is your emphasis on the relevance of

EXERCISE Roots of Disempowerment

early disempowering experiences to the present. It is crucial for you to help participants build the bridge between early experiences and current feelings of disempowerment in their agencies. Anything from the past that contributes to participants' feeling unworthy, incompetent, insecure, and uncertain will influence participants' feelings of impotence as change agents. For example, if a participant talks about not feeling worthy or competent after not being chosen for the A team, the trainer might explore the possibility that experiences like this one contribute to the participant's not feeling competent or worthy enough to make a difference in changing practices in the agency. This example is not given to suggest a linear cause and effect. Rather, participants are encouraged to reflect on the impact of early experiences on feeling disempowered as change agents.

Lead the group through the following steps:

1. Think back to your childhood and teenage years. Recall a time when you felt overwhelmed, disempowered, or too small to tackle a problem. It is helpful to think of the earliest experience possible. Be mindful of your mental and emotional health and focus on a specific event you have mostly healed from and are willing to share with the group. You will have a little time now without interruption to recall a specific incident.

2. Pair up with one other person. Each of you will have 3–5 minutes to tell your story to your partner. When time is called, the first speaker finishes and the second speaker begins.

After this part of the exercise is finished, lead the group through the second section as follows:

1. Do a short debriefing by asking participants to share the feelings elicited by the telling of their story. Remind participants that it is important to focus on the feelings that came up and not on the stories themselves. Ask questions such as: What feelings came up for you as you told your story? What was it like for you to tell your story?

2. Ask the group members to reflect on the stories and think about how oppression contributed to them. What elements of sexism, classism, racism, ableism, ageism, or other prejudicial attitudes may have been a part of your story?

3. Ask for a volunteer to share his or her story with the group. Sit next to the volunteer as a way of offering support. Instruct the volunteer as follows: "Take a minute to collect your thoughts. When you are ready to begin, tell your story to the group." Participants stay focused on the volunteer during the entire time. There is no time limit placed on the volunteer. When the

80 FUTURE ACTION

EXERCISE Roots of Disempowerment

volunteer has finished, ask participants to show their appreciation of the story by giving the volunteer a round of applause.

4. Say the following to the volunteer: "In order to relearn a useful lesson from this experience, I would like you to find your voice around the story you just told. I want you to speak to the incident as an adult who is looking back on this disempowering experience. For example, how did the incident affect you as a child? What conclusions did you draw from the experience? How does the incident continue to have an impact on you today? How might you respond differently?" After the volunteer's comments, the group shows its appreciation once again.

Processing

Debrief the group by asking the following questions:

- What feelings came up for you?
- What was it like for you to listen to the volunteer's story?
- What similarities do you see to your own story?
- What are your thoughts about how oppression and privilege are part of the disempowering experience?

If time allows, ask another volunteer to tell his or her story to the group. Although time limits this exercise to several volunteers, other participants relate to the volunteers from their own backgrounds and become reflective about their own early experiences. Highlight that the conclusions drawn by the volunteers from earlier parts of their lives are largely responsible for their predictable reactions in the face of clearly needed changes in the agency.

Some examples of conclusions include the following:

- "If I stand out, I'll get picked on."
- "I shouldn't try because I never do it right anyway."
- "I don't know enough to justify what I am feeling."

These conclusions induce feelings of being overwhelmed, impotent, discounted, blamed, and so on that "disempower" participants from taking risks in their agencies.

MINI LECTURE Changing Perspectives: The Agency as Your Client

Mini Lecture
Changing Perspectives: The Agency as Your Client

Objective
The purpose of this mini lecture is to increase the ability of participants to become active change agents by altering their perceptions of the agency's omnipotence and their own limited power. Having reevaluated the impact of disempowering experiences, participants are able to consider different attitudes and approaches that will advance their roles as social change agents and advocates for multicultural competence. The concepts are borrowed from Lawrence Shulman (1992). Note: Use the word "social worker" or the pronoun "you" or "we" depending on the tone you prefer to emphasize.

Instructions
Lead the group through the following lecture.

Content
Usually the social worker thinks of the agency in a hierarchical arrangement. The agency is on top, the social worker comes next, and under the social worker are clients. What would happen if the social worker changed that arrangement and made it horizontal with the social worker in the middle and the agency and client on either end? What would happen if the social worker began to realize that both the agency and the client are clients? Indeed, the social worker has two clients to attend to—the client who comes to the agency and the agency itself. Both have problems and both need help.

The client who comes to the agency may need help with money for groceries. The agency client needs help in becoming more responsive to the needs of a *diverse* clientele. Like an involuntary client, the agency may not recognize that it needs help. How would the social worker respond differently if he or she thought of the agency that way? The social worker might do an assessment. The social worker might develop a treatment plan based on the assessment. The social worker might think about how he or she was going to gain the client's trust. The social worker might think about how the client will react to change and what the social worker has to do to reduce the client's resistance. The social worker might think about whom he or she would go to for ongoing supervision or consultation about a difficult client.

If the social worker starts to think about the agency as a client, he or she might even have some compassion for what it takes to make change happen, how

82 FUTURE ACTION

MINI LECTURE Changing Perspectives: The Agency as Your Client

scared clients are to try out new behaviors, or how much support is needed to stabilize change. It is also important to remember that clients change at different rates, and an ample amount of repetition is needed to make change happen and solidify. As we think about the agency as a client, it shifts the social worker's status as well as the status of the agency. The arrangement is no longer hierarchical with the agency on top and the social worker at the bottom of the stack. Now the arrangement is more horizontal, and perhaps even collaborative, which allows the agency to be experienced as less intimidating.

Ask the participants to consider the following questions in order to move toward positive change in their agencies:

- What is my psychosocial assessment of the problem?
- What is the treatment plan?
- What kind of initiative do I need to take?
- What stages must the agency-client go through?
- What kind of resistance can I expect from my agency-client?
- How do I manage the resistance?
- Do I need outside supervision/consultation to deal with agency-client's resistance?
- What kind of follow-up is necessary?

Then continue the lecture with the following discussion:

Viewing the agency as client requires a paradigm shift. When viewed in this way, however, the difficulty of bringing about agency change may be seen as a normal part of the helping process. Agencies don't have all the answers in the same way that clients don't have all the answers. Yet agency-clients seek change, too. You, as social workers, are encouraged to visualize your role in the agency from a horizontal perspective. The social worker is the conduit that moves between the client community and the agency administration. Both entities truly need the social worker's help. Moreover, believing in and working from this perspective challenges the disempowering beliefs that keep the social worker small and stop him or her from taking effective action relative to issues of cultural and social diversity.

Additionally, it may be helpful to think about the various ways that the agency experiences oppression and privilege. For example, in what ways does society's sexism contribute to the disempowerment of a domestic violence shelter via the following channels?

- Lack of funding
- Lack of visibility of the social problems targeted by the agency
- Lack of laws or regulations that facilitate the work of the agency

Challenge the participants to think about the various ways that oppression can be manifested in this broad, societal scale.

Conclusion

Closing activities for the last session are more extensive than for the previous sessions. They include three activities:

1. Agreement With Self
2. Verbal Evaluation About the Training
3. Words of Inspiration

These activities help participants to

- Integrate all the material that has been presented in the training
- Give the training team feedback about what was helpful, challenging, or irrelevant

Agreement With Self

Participants complete a one-page form describing the changes they are planning to make as a result of the training. A copy of the form can be found in appendix E. Changes may include personal aspects about participants in relation to cultural and social diversity, decisions to risk attention to differences and social inequities in student supervision, and/or actions to have an impact on the multicultural competence of the agency. Remind participants to be realistic about what they can and cannot do, that change happens in stages. Participants hand in the Agreement With Self at the end of this meeting. Return this Agreement With Self to the participant at the end of six months with a letter of reminder, also in appendix E. The return of the Agreement With Self after six months helps participants hold themselves accountable to their commitments.

Verbal Evaluation

The verbal evaluation brings the training to a close. The discussion is loosely structured to allow participants to offer feedback on the training as a whole, provide feedback to trainers, speak about their gains, make observations about the contributions of other participants, and so forth. Specifically, ask participants to give their opinions about what was uncomfortable and comfortable for them. Comments may include the following:

- "It was hard to disclose my own gaps and biases."
- "I don't know about people with disabilities."

- "I enjoyed the camaraderie and in a small group I felt safe and empowered."
- "I want to work on my tendency to be overly solicitous with African American males."

Participants may give each other suggestions for change. This feedback provides both you and the participants with a clear picture of the strengths and weaknesses of the Collaborative Training Model.

Words of Inspiration

Read parting words of inspiration to the participants as a way of thanking them for their contributions and wishing them well. Examples of parting words of inspiration can be found in many sources, such as *Chicken Soup for the Soul*, other self-help books, and the sacred writings of various religious groups. (See appendix E.) It is important to read words of inspiration that are secular in their tone and inclusive of diverse groups.

PART 5

Wrap-Up

CHAPTER 12

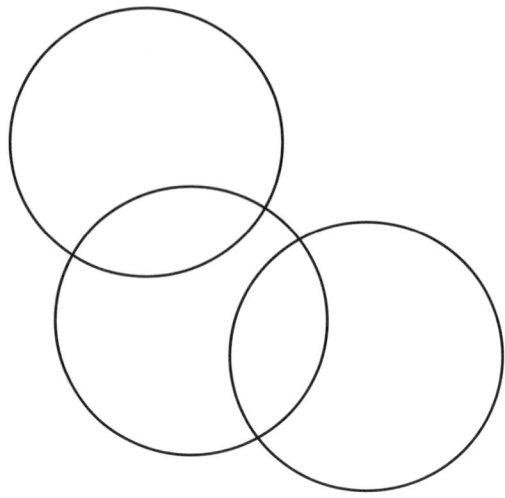

Closing Statement

The Collaborative Training Model is divided into three themes that reflect the real world where field instructors work and teach. The themes grow and develop one from another in an expanding circle of influence. The themes focus on the following:

1. Relationship With Self
2. Relationship With Student Supervisee
3. Relationship With Agency

The Collaborative Model is a psychological intervention to address manifestations of avoidance in all themes with the goal of enabling field instructors to be more effective teachers. It offers to selected field instructors a group experience in which issues of diversity are addressed purposefully and directly. In this model, participants are encouraged to verbalize the anxiety and avoidance that is a natural part of dealing with issues of race, ethnicity, class, sexual orientation, and other important differences. Trainers are to be gentle and persistent in attending to the exploration and expression of participants' anxiety and the thoughts and feelings that generate it. Skills are offered to help field instructors tolerate and push through this anxiety and avoidance to reach for a deeper understanding of themselves and the dynamics surrounding the situations they find themselves in. This process sets the stage for field instructors to integrate knowledge about social and cultural diversity and social justice into the social work students' field experience.

The Collaborative Model takes advantage of one of the mainstays in the social work profession—the importance of relationships. Participants grow and develop through the relationships they form with each other and with members of the training team. The training helps participants cultivate and nurture these relationships and the realization that they are not alone in struggling with the tough issues that surface within themselves, with the social work students they supervise, and at their agencies. They learn that others have the same feelings of anxiety, avoidance, and being overwhelmed that they have endured. Their experiences are validated. They discover that they can consult with each other and discuss past successes and triumphs. These relationships have a transformational effect on the entire group, including the training team members.

The overall justification for this training is multifaceted. It is rooted in the knowledge that the demographics of our country are changing. The change in population growth from 1990 to 2000 was the largest in American history, with a dramatic increase in people of color from 20 to 25 percent (Perry & Mackum, 2001). Immigration is deemed the determinant factor in U.S. population growth (Camarota, 2001). Roughly 40 percent of the nearly 33 million increase in the size of the U.S. population during the 1990s is directly attributable to the arrival of new immigrants. Because of the aging of the baby boomer generation, the elderly population is expected to more than double, representing 20 percent of the population by 2030 (Centers for Disease Control and Prevention, 2003). These trends have been noted by demographers for many years and are likely to continue. The changing demographics bring social workers to the forefront of issues of cultural competency. Often, social workers work with people who are in crisis or in need of outside help. In order to be effective helpers, we must be self-aware, have culture-specific knowledge and skills, and be leaders in issues of social and economic justice.

The developmental nature of the Collaborative Training Model facilitates the growth of field instructors to be effective teachers. This, in turn, facilitates the growth of social work interns to be effective in their work with clients. The group intervention with field instructors parallels the individual "intervention"/education that field instructors offer their students.

The developers of this manual are genuinely interested in having others experience its effectiveness with field instructors in other parts of the country. Please contact any of the developers to consult further on this work. The developers are:

Marilyn Armour, PhD, LICSW, assistant professor

Bonnie Bain, LCSW, clinical professor

Ruth Rubio, LMSW-AP, clinical professor

All three professors can be reached at this address: University of Texas, Austin, School of Social Work, 1 University Station, D3500, Austin, Texas 78712.

References

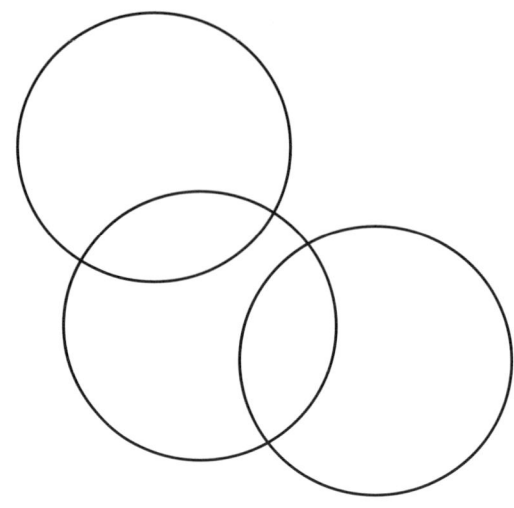

Arkin, N. (1999). Culturally sensitive student supervision: Difficulties and challenges. *Clinical Supervisor, 18*, 1–16.

Armour, M. P., Bain, B., & Rubio, R. (2004). Evaluation study of diversity training for field instructors: A collaborative approach to avoidant behavior. *Journal of Social Work Education, 40*, 27–37.

Bailey, D., & Aronoff, N. (2004). The integration of multicultural competency and organizational practice in social work education. In L. Gutiérrez, M. E. Zuñiga, & D. Lum (Eds.), *Education for multicultural social work practice: Critical viewpoints and future directions* (pp. 135–144). Alexandria, VA: Council on Social Work Education.

Bain, B., & Garcia, E. (1999, February). *Field education: Opportunities for expanding vision and competency in working with diversity*. Paper presented at the 45th Annual Program Meeting, Council on Social Work Education, New York.

Bell, L. A. (1997). Theoretical foundations for social justice education. In M. Adams, L. A. Bell, & P. Griffin (Eds.), *Teaching for diversity and social justice: A sourcebook* (pp. 3–15). New York: Routledge.

Bogo, M. (1993). The student/field instructor relationship: The critical factor in field education. *Clinical Supervisor, 16*, 39–54.

Camarota, S. (2001). The impact of immigration on U.S. population growth. Testimony prepared for the U.S. House of Representatives Committee on the Judiciary Subcommittee on Immigration, Border Security, and Claims. Center for Immigration Studies. August 2, 2001. Retrieved October 15, 2005, from http://www.cis.org/articles/2001/sactestimony701.html

Carrillo, D. F., Holzhalb, C. M., & Thyer, B. A. (1993). Assessing social work students' attitudes related to cultural diversity: A review of selected measures. *Journal of Social Work Education, 29*, 263–268.

Cashwell, C. S., Looby, E. J., & Housley, W. (1997). Appreciating cultural diversity through clinical supervision. *Clinical Supervisor, 15*, 75–85.

Centers for Disease Control and Prevention. (2003). Public health and aging: Trends in aging—United States and worldwide. *Morbidity and Mortality Weekly Report, 52*, 101–106. Retrieved October 15, 2005, from http://www.cdc.gov/mmwr/preview/mmwrhtml/mm5206a2.htm

Chan, C. S., & Treacy, M. J. (1996). Resistance in multicultural courses: Student, faculty, and classroom dynamics. *American Behavioral Scientist, 40*, 212–221.

Cross, T., Bazron, B., Dennis, K. W., & Isaacs, M. R. (1989). *Towards a culturally competent system of care, volume I.* Washington, DC: CASSP Technical Assistance Center at Georgetown University Child Development Center.

Dean, R. G., & Fleck-Henderson, A. (1992). Teaching clinical theory and practice through a constructivist lens. *Journal of Teaching in Social Work, 6*, 3–20.

Doehrman, M. J. (1976). Parallel processes in supervision and psychotherapy. *Bulletin of the Menninger Clinic, 40*, 1–104.

Dore, M. M. (1993). The practice-teaching parallel in educating the micropractitioner. *Journal of Social Work Education, 29*, 181–190.

Fong, R. (Ed.) (2004). *Culturally competent practice with immigrant and refugee children and families.* New York: Guilford Press.

Fong, R., & Furuto, S. (2001). *Culturally competent practice: Skills, interventions, and evaluations.* Boston: Allyn & Bacon.

Fong, R., & Lum, D. (2004). Developing an integrated model of cultural competency in social work education. In L. Gutiérrez, M. Zuñiga, & D. Lum (Eds.), *Education for social work practice: Critical views and new directions* (pp. 19–30). Alexandria, VA: Council on Social Work Education.

Freeman, M. L., & Valentine, D. (1998). The connected classroom: Modeling the evaluation of practice by evaluating the classroom group. *Journal of Teaching in Social Work, 17*, 15–29.

Garcia, B., & Van Soest, D. (1999). Teaching about diversity and oppression: Learning from the analysis of critical classroom events. *Journal of Teaching in Social Work, 18*, 149–167.

Giroux, H. (1996). *Living dangerously: Multiculturalism and the politics of difference.* New York: Lang.

Gladstein, M., & Mailick, M. (1986). An affirmative approach to ethnic diversity in field work. *Journal of Social Work Education, 22*, 41–49.

Gutiérrez, L., & Nagda, B. (1996). The multicultural imperative in human service organizations. In R. Raffoul and C. McNeece (Eds.), *Future issues in social work practice* (pp. 203–213). Boston: Allyn & Bacon.

Gutiérrez, L., Zuñiga, M. E., & Lum, D. (Eds.). (2004). *Education for multicultural social work practice: Critical viewpoints and future directions.* Alexandria, VA: Council on Social Work Education.

Helms, J. E., & Cook, D. A. (1999). *Using race and culture in counseling and psychotherapy.* Boston: Allyn & Bacon.

Hendricks, C. O. (2003). Learning and teaching cultural competence in the practice of social work. *Journal of Teaching in Social Work, 23,* 73–86.

Holley, L. G., & Steiner, S. (2005). Safe space: Student perspectives on classroom environment. *Journal of Social Work Education, 41,* 49–64.

Hyde, C., & Ruth, B. (2002). Multicultural content and class participation. Do students self-censor? *Journal of Social Work Education, 38,* 241–256.

Julia, M. (2000). Student perceptions of culture: An integral part of social work practice. *International Journal of Cultural Relations, 24*(2), 279–289.

Kaiser, T. (1997). *Supervisory relationships: Exploring the human element.* Pacific Grove, CA: Brooks/Cole.

Kim, H., & Leong, F. (1991). Going beyond cultural sensitivity on the road to multiculturalism: Using the Intercultural Sensitizer as a counselor training tool. *Journal of Counseling and Development, 70,* 112–118.

Leong, F. T. L., & Wagner, N. S. (1994). Cross-cultural counseling supervision: What do we know? What do we need to know? *Counselor Education and Supervision, 34,* 117–131.

Lum, D. (1999). *Culturally competent practice: A framework for growth and action.* Pacific Grove, CA: Brooks/Cole.

Lum, D. (2003). *Culturally competent practice: A framework for growth and action* (2nd ed.). Pacific Grove, CA: Brooks/Cole.

Lum, D. (2005). *Cultural competence, practice stages and client systems: A case study approach.* Belmont, CA: Thomson/Brooks/Cole.

Manoleas, P. (2004). The field practicum as the focus point for training diversity-competent MSW social workers. In L. Gutiérrez, M. E. Zuñiga, & D. Lum (Eds.), *Education for multicultural social work practice: Critical viewpoints and future directions* (pp. 237–250). Alexandria, VA: Council on Social Work Education.

Marshack, E., Hendricks, C. O., & Gladstein, M. (1994). The commonality of difference: Teaching about diversity in field instruction. *Journal of Multicultural Social Work, 3*(1), 77–89.

McChesney, M., & Euster, G. L. (2000). Evaluation of an active learning method for field instructor training. *Journal of Teaching in Social Work, 20,* 201–215.

McIntosh, P. (1993). White privilege and male privilege: A personal account of coming to see correspondences through work in women's studies. In A. Minas (Ed.), *Gender basics: Feminist perspectives in women and men* (pp. 30–38). Belmont, CA: Wadsworth.

McMahon, A., & Allen-Meares, P. (1992). Is social work racist? A content analysis of recent literature. *Social Work, 37,* 533–539.

McRoy, R. G., Freeman, E. M., Logan, S. L., & Blackmon, B. (1986). Cross-cultural field supervision: Implications for social work education. *Journal of Social Work Education, 22,* 50–55.

Miller, J., Hyde, C., & Ruth, B. J. (2004). Teaching about race and racism in social work: The challenge for white educators. *Smith College Studies in Social Work, 74,* 409–426.

Mishna, F., & Rasmussen, B. (2001).The learning relationship: Working through disjunctions in the classroom. *Clinical Social Work Journal, 29,* 387–399.

National Association of Social Workers. (1999). *Code of ethics.* Washington, DC: Author.

National Association of Social Workers. (2001). *NASW standards for cultural competence in social work practice.* Washington, DC: Author.

Perry, M. J., & Mackum, P. J. (2001). Population change and distribution: 1990–2000. *Census 2000 brief*, April 2, 2001. Retrieved June 28, 2001, from http://www.census.gov/prod/ 2001pubs/c2kbr01-2.pdf

Peterson, M. (1986). *Parallel process in field instruction.* Paper presented at the Annual Field Workers Conference, University of Minnesota, Minneapolis, MN.

Peterson, M. (1992). *At personal risk: Boundary violations in professional and client relationships.* New York: W. W. Norton.

Pinderhughes, E. (1989). *Understanding race, ethnicity and power: The key to efficacy in clinical practice.* New York: Free Press.

Porter, N. (1994). Empowering supervisors to empower others: A culturally responsive supervision model. *Hispanic Journal of Behavioral Sciences, 16,* 43–56.

Priddy, W. W. (2004). Multicultural competence in the field practicum. In L. Gutiérrez, M. E. Zuñiga, & D. Lum (Eds.), *Education for multicultural social work practice: Critical viewpoints and future directions* (pp. 237–250). Alexandria, VA: Council on Social Work Education.

Raske, M. (1999). Using feminist classroom rules to model empowerment for social work students. *Journal of Teaching in Social Work, 19,* 197–208.

Ryan, A., & Hendricks, C. (1989). Culture and communication: Supervising the Asian and Hispanic social worker. *Clinical Supervisor, 7,* 27–40

Shulman, L. (1992). *Interactional supervision.* Washington, DC: NASW Press.

Solomon, B. (1982). Power: The troublesome factor in cross-cultural supervision. *Smith College School of Social Work Journal, 10*(1), 27–32.

Torres, J., & Jones, J. (1997). You've got to be taught: Multicultural education for social workers. *Journal of Teaching in Social Work, 15,* 161–179.

Van Soest, D. (2004). Structural barriers to multicultural competence in the field practicum. In L. Gutiérrez, M. E. Zuñiga, & D. Lum (Eds.), *Education for multicultural social work practice: Critical viewpoints and future directions* (pp. 265–278). Alexandria, VA: Council on Social Work Education.

Van Soest, D., & Garcia, B. (2003). *Diversity education for social justice: Mastering teaching skills.* Alexandria, VA: Council on Social Work Education.

Walters, G. M., Strom-Gottfried, K. J., & Sullivan, M. (1998). Assembling the pieces in the diversity puzzle: A field model. *Journal of Social Work Education, 34,* 353–363.

Appendix A

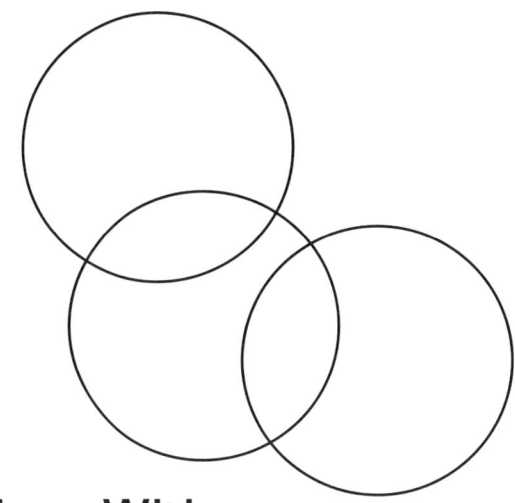

Seven Formats: Full and Modified Designs With Consecutive and Intermittent Schedules

Introduction to Formats

On the following pages, you will find seven formats outlined. Each of formats 1 through 7 stands alone as a training to be considered for implementation. As you review each of the seven formats, you can consider the unique circumstances of your institution, city, resources available, and so on, in order to determine the option that best addresses the your situation. The formats do not overlap. Figures show a visual depiction of the overall training effort based on different formats. Tables illustrate sessions and timetables with designated topics for discussion/presentation.

FIGURE 1

Format 1 (Consecutive) and Format 2 (Intermittent)
Full Model: 3 Six-Hour Sessions

TRAINERS' MEETINGS	TRAINING	MODULES
Meeting #1	Session #1 *Give RQ*	Relationship With Self
Meeting #2	Session #2 *Turn in RQ* *Give new RQ*	Relationship With Student Supervisee
Meeting #3 *Review RQ*	Session #3 *Turn in RQ*	Relationship With Agency
Meeting #4 *Review RQ*		

RQ=Reflecting Questions

TABLE 3
Format 1 (Consecutive) and Format 2 (Intermittent) Full Model: 3 Six-Hour Sessions

TOPIC		TIME ALLOTMENT[1]
RELATIONSHIP WITH SELF		
Module 1: Welcoming Diversity in Self		3 hours
Introduction		15 minutes
Exercise 1: Icebreaker		60 minutes
Mini Lecture: Normalization of Anxiety		10 minutes
Mini Lecture: Orientation to the Training		10 minutes
Exercise 2: Weaving a Tapestry		20 minutes
Exercise 3: Internalized Attitudes		30 minutes
Exercise 4: Reclaiming Dignity and Honor		20 minutes
Conclusion		20 minutes
	Total	185 minutes
Reflecting Questions (Lunch)		*60 minutes*
Module 2: Taking a Stand for Diversity		3 hours
Introduction		5 minutes
Round-Robin Responses		60 minutes
Mini Lecture: Diving Deeper		10 minutes
Exercise 1: Taking Power Back		20 minutes
Break		*10 minutes*
Exercise 2: Reevaluation		45 minutes
Conclusion		30 minutes
	Total	180 minutes
Reflecting Questions		
RELATIONSHIP WITH STUDENT SUPERVISEE		
Module 3: Exploring Diversity in the Supervisory Relationship		3 hours
Introduction and Round-Robin Responses		80 minutes
Mini Lecture: Parallel Process		10 minutes
Mini Lecture: Power		30 minutes
Mini Lecture: Boundaries		20 minutes
Exercise: Exploring Dilemmas		20 minutes
Conclusion		20 minutes
	Total	180 minutes
Reflecting Questions (Lunch)		*60 minutes*

RELATIONSHIP WITH STUDENT SUPERVISEE (Continued)

Module 4: Effecting Change in the Supervisory Relationship — 3 hours
Introduction — 10 minutes
Round-Robin Responses — 40 minutes
Exercise 1: Role Playing — 15 minutes
Exercise 2: Group Consultation — 40 minutes
Exercise 3: Reconvened Role Playing — 35 minutes
Mini Lecture: Didactic Handout — 25 minutes
Conclusion — 15 minutes
Total — 180 minutes

Reflecting Questions

RELATIONSHIP WITH AGENCY

Module 5: Diversity and Your Agency — 3 hours
Introduction and Round-Robin Responses — 45 minutes
Mini Lecture: Cultural Competence Continuum — 15 minutes
Exercise: Agency Assessment — 55 minutes
Conclusion — 45 minutes
Total — 160 minutes

Reflecting Questions — 60 minutes

Module 6: Future Action — 3 hours
Introduction — 10 minutes
Round-Robin Responses — 10 minutes
Mini Lecture: Disempowerment — 25 minutes
Exercise: Roots of Disempowerment — 60 minutes
Mini Lecture: Changing Perspectives: The Agency as Your Client — 35 minutes
Conclusion — 40 minutes
Total — 180 minutes

---

[1] Alloted time for each module is approximate and may not take 3 hours.

96 APPENDIX A

FIGURE 2
Format 3 (Intermittent)
Full Model: 6 Three-Hour Sessions

TRAINERS' MEETINGS	TRAINING	MODULES
Meeting #1	Session #1 *Give RQ*	Relationship With Self
Meeting #2	Session #2 *Turn in RQ* *Give new RQ*	
Meeting #3 *Review RQ*	Session #3 *Turn in RQ* *Give new RQ*	Relationship With Student Supervisee
Meeting #4 *Review RQ*	Session #4 *Turn in RQ* *Give new RQ*	
Meeting #5 *Review RQ*	Session #5 *Turn in RQ* *Give new RQ*	Relationship With Agency
Meeting #6 *Review RQ*	Session #6 *Turn in RQ*	
Meeting #7 *Review RQ*		

RQ=Reflecting Questions

TABLE 4
Format 3 (Intermittent)
Full Model: 6 Three-Hour Sessions

TOPIC		TIME ALLOTMENT[1]
RELATIONSHIP WITH SELF		
Module 1: Welcoming Diversity in Self		3 hours
Introduction		15 minutes
Exercise 1: Icebreaker		60 minutes
Mini Lecture: Normalization of Anxiety		15 minutes
Mini Lecture: Orientation to the Training		10 minutes
Exercise 2: Weaving a Tapestry		20 minutes
Exercise 3: Internalized Attitudes		30 minutes
Exercise 4: Reclaiming Dignity and Honor		20 minutes
Conclusion		20 minutes
Reflecting Questions		
	Total	190 minutes
Module 2: Taking a Stand for Diversity		3 hours
Introduction		5 minutes
Round-Robin Responses		60 minutes
Mini Lecture: Diving Deeper		10 minutes
Exercise 1: Taking Power Back		20 minutes
Break		*10 minutes*
Exercise 2: Reevaluation		45 minutes
Conclusion		30 minutes
Reflecting Questions		
	Total	180 minutes
RELATIONSHIP WITH STUDENT SUPERVISEE		
Module 3: Exploring Diversity in the Supervisory Relationship		3 hours
Introduction and Round-Robin Responses		80 minutes
Mini Lecture: Parallel Process		10 minutes
Mini Lecture: Power		20–30 minutes
Mini Lecture: Boundaries		20 minutes
Exercise: Exploring Dilemmas		20 minutes
Conclusion		20 minutes
Reflecting Questions		
	Total	170–180 minutes

(Continued)

TABLE 4 (*Continued*)
Format 3 (Intermittent)
Full Model: 6 Three-Hour Sessions

TOPIC	TIME ALLOTMENT
RELATIONSHIP WITH STUDENT SUPERVISEE (Continued)	
Module 4: Effecting Change in the Supervisory Relationship	3 hours
Introduction	10 minutes
Round-Robin Responses	40 minutes
Exercise 1: Role Playing	15 minutes
Exercise 2: Group Consultation	40 minutes
Exercise 3: Reconvened Role Playing	35 minutes
Mini Lecture: Didactic Handout	25 minutes
Conclusion	15 minutes
Reflecting Questions	
Total	180 minutes
RELATIONSHIP WITH AGENCY	
Module 5: Diversity and Your Agency	3 hours
Introduction and Round-Robin Responses	45 minutes
Mini Lecture: Cultural Competence Continuum	15 minutes
Exercise: Agency Assessment	55 minutes
Conclusion	45 minutes
Total	160 minutes
Reflecting Questions	*60 minutes*
Module 6: Future Action	3 hours
Introduction	10 minutes
Round-Robin Responses	25 minutes
Mini Lecture: Disempowerment	10 minutes
Exercise: Roots of Disempowerment	60 minutes
Mini Lecture: Changing Perspectives: The Agency as Your Client	35 minutes
Conclusion	40 minutes
Total	180 minutes

[1] Alloted time for each module is approximate and may not take 3 hours.

FIGURE 3
Format 4 (Consecutive) and Format 5 (Intermittent)
Modified: 2 Sessions. Session 1: 6 Hours; Session 2: 8 Hours

TRAINERS' MEETINGS	TRAINING	MODULES
Meeting #1	Session #1 *Give RQ*	Relationship With Self Relationship With Student Supervisee I
Meeting #2	Session #2 *Turn in RQ*	Relationship With Student Supervisee II
Meeting #3 *Review RQ*		Relationship With Agency

RQ=Reflecting Questions

TABLE 5
Format 4 (Consecutive) and Format 5 (Intermittent) Modified: 2 Sessions. Session 1: 6 Hours; Session 2: 8 Hours

TOPIC		TIME ALLOTMENT
SESSION 1		
RELATIONSHIP WITH SELF		
Module 1: Welcoming Diversity in Self		2.5 hours
Introduction		10 minutes
Exercise 1: Icebreaker		55 minutes
Mini Lecture: Normalization of Anxiety		10 minutes
Mini Lecture: Orientation to the Training		10 minutes
Exercise 2: Weaving a Tapestry		15 minutes
Exercise 3: Internalized Attitudes		20 minutes
Exercise 4: Reclaiming Dignity and Honor		15 minutes
Conclusion		15 minutes
	Total	150 minutes
Reflecting Questions (lunch)		*60 minutes*
Module 2: Taking a Stand for Diversity		1.5 hours
Introduction		5 minutes
Round-Robin Responses		10 minutes
Mini Lecture: Diving Deeper		10 minutes
Exercise 1: Taking Power Back		15 minutes
Exercise 2: Reevaluation		20 minutes
Conclusion		15 minutes
Reflecting Questions		*15 minutes*
	Total	90 minutes
Break		*10 minutes*
RELATIONSHIP WITH STUDENT SUPERVISEE I		
Module 3: Exploring Diversity in the Supervisory Relationship		2 hours
Introduction and Round-Robin Responses		40 minutes
Mini Lecture: Parallel Process		10 minutes
Mini Lecture: Power		30 minutes
Mini Lecture: Boundaries		10 minutes
Exercise: Exploring Dilemmas		20 minutes
Conclusion		10 minutes
	Total	120 minutes
Reflecting Questions		

(Continued)

TOPIC	TIME ALLOTMENT
SESSION 2	
RELATIONSHIP WITH STUDENT SUPERVISEE II	
Module 4: Effecting Change in the Supervisory Relationship	3 hours
Introduction	10 minutes
Round-Robin Responses	40 minutes
Exercise 1: Role Playing	15 minutes
Exercise 2: Group Consultation	40 minutes
Exercise 3: Reconvened Role Playing	15 minutes
Processing	20 minutes
Mini Lecture: Didactic Handout	25 minutes
Conclusion	15 minutes
Total	180 minutes
Reflecting Questions	*60 minutes*
RELATIONSHIP WITH AGENCY	
Module 5: Diversity and Your Agency	2 hours
Introduction and Round-Robin Responses	30 minutes
Mini Lecture: Cultural Competence Continuum	15 minutes
Exercise: Agency Assessment	45 minutes
Conclusion	30 minutes
Total	120 minutes
Break	*15 minutes*
Module 6: Future Action	3 hours
Introduction	10 minutes
Round-Robin Responses	35 minutes
Mini Lecture: Disempowerment	10 minutes
Exercise: Roots of Disempowerment	60 minutes
Break	*15 minutes*
Mini Lecture: Changing Perspectives: The Agency as Your Client	35 minutes
Conclusion	30 minutes
Total	180 minutes

FIGURE 4
Format 6 (Consecutive) and Format 7 (Intermittent)
Modified: 3 Sessions
Session 1: 4 Hours; Session 2: 5 Hours; Session 3: 5 Hours

TRAINERS' MEETINGS	TRAINING	MODULES
Meeting #1	Session #1 *Give RQ*	Relationship With Self
Meeting #2	Session #2 *Turn in RQ* *Give New RQ*	Relationship With Student Supervisee
Meeting #3 *Review RQ*	Session #3 *Turn in RQ*	Relationship With Agency
Meeting #4 *Review RQ*		

RQ=Reflecting Questions

TABLE 6
Format 6 (Consecutive) and Format 7 (Intermittent)
Modified: 3 Sessions
Session 1: 4 Hours; Session 2: 5 Hours; Session 3: 5 Hours

TOPIC		TIME ALLOTMENT
SESSION 1		
RELATIONSHIP WITH SELF		
Module 1: Welcoming Diversity in Self		2.5 hours
Introduction		10 minutes
Exercise 1: Icebreaker		55 minutes
Mini Lecture: Normalization of Anxiety		10 minutes
Mini Lecture: Orientation to the Training		10 minutes
Exercise 2: Weaving a Tapestry		15 minutes
Exercise 3: Internalized Attitudes		20 minutes
Exercise 4: Reclaiming Dignity and Honor		15 minutes
Conclusion		15 minutes
Reflecting Questions		*15 minutes*
	Total	150 minutes
Break		*15 minutes*
Module 2: Taking a Stand for Diversity		1.5 hours
Introduction		5 minutes
Round-Robin Responses		10 minutes
Mini Lecture: Diving Deeper		10 minutes
Exercise 1: Taking Power Back		15 minutes
Exercise 2: Reevaluation		20 minutes
Conclusion		30 minutes
	Total	90 minutes
Reflecting Questions		
SESSION 2		
RELATIONSHIP WITH STUDENT SUPERVISEE		
Module 3: Exploring Diversity in the Supervisory Relationship		2 hours
Introduction and Round-Robin Responses		40 minutes
Mini Lecture: Parallel Process		10 minutes
Mini Lecture: Power		30 minutes
Mini Lecture: Boundaries		10 minutes
Exercise: Exploring Dilemmas		20 minutes
Conclusion		10 minutes
	Total	120 minutes
Reflecting Questions		20 minutes

(Continued)

TABLE 6
SESSION 2 (Continued)

TOPIC		TIME ALLOTMENT
Module 4: Effecting Change in the Supervisory Relationship		3 hours
Introduction		10 minutes
Round-Robin Responses		40 minutes
Exercise 1: Role Playing		15 minutes
Exercise 2: Group Consultation		40 minutes
Exercise 3: Reconvened Role Playing		35 minutes
Mini Lecture: Didactic Handout		25 minutes
Conclusion		15 minutes
	Total	180 minutes

Reflecting Questions

SESSION 3

RELATIONSHIP WITH AGENCY

Module 5: Diversity and Your Agency		2 hours
Introduction and Round-Robin Responses		30 minutes
Mini Lecture: Cultural Competence Continuum		15 minutes
Exercise: Agency Assessment		45 minutes
Conclusion		30 minutes
	Total	120 minutes
Break		*15 minutes*
Module 6: Future Action		3 hours
Introduction		10 minutes
Round-Robin Responses		35 minutes
Mini Lecture: Disempowerment		10 minutes
Exercise: Roots of Disempowerment		60 minutes
Break		*15 minutes*
Mini Lecture: Changing Perspectives: The Agency as Your Client		20 minutes
Conclusion		30 minutes
	Total	180 minutes

TABLE 7
18-Hour Full Design
Consecutive and Intermittent Schedules

SESSION AND CONTENT

Relationship With Self	6 hours
Relationship With Student Supervisee	6 hours
Relationship With Agency	6 hours
Total	18 hours

1 Consecutive Schedule

- **PROs** Intensifies impact
  Retention increased
  Continuity of group process enhanced
  Retreat format promotes informal exchanges

- **CONs** Increased fatigue and vulnerability
  Fatigue of trainers
  Lack of time for integration and individual processing
  Less time to build cross-cultural comfort, safety, and trust
  Lack of planning time between sessions

2 Intermittent Schedule; 3 Intermittent Format

- **PROs** Process over time increases depth and integration
  Heightens quality of group process over time
  Attention to the developmental nature of the training
  Opportunity to experiment with new knowledge
  Opportunity to alter training location
  Planning time between sessions

- **CONs** Retention issues may arise
  Loss of momentum due to time lapse between sessions

TABLE 8
14-Hour Modified Model
Consecutive and Intermittent Schedules

2 SESSIONS

Day 1		7 hours
Day 2		7 hours
	Total	14 hours

CONTENT

Relationship With Self		4 hours
Relationship With Student Supervisee		5 hours
Relationship With Agency		5 hours
	Total	14 hours

4 Consecutive Schedule

- **PROs** Intensifies impact
  Retention increased
  Continuity of group process enhanced
  Retreat format promotes informal exchanges

- **CONs** Increased fatigue and vulnerability
  Fatigue of trainers
  Lack of time for integration and individual processing
  Less time to build cross-cultural comfort, safety, and trust
  Lack of planning time between sessions

5 Intermittent Schedule

- **PROs** Opportunity to experiment with new knowledge
  Adequate planning time between sessions

- **CONs** Retention issues may arise
  Loss of momentum due to time lapse between sessions

(Continued)

3 SESSIONS

Day 1	4 hours
Day 2	5 hours
Day 3	5 hours
Total	14 hours

CONTENT

Relationship With Self	4 hours
Relationship With Student Supervisee	5 hours
Relationship With Agency	5 hours
Total	14 hours

6 Consecutive Schedule

PROs Intensifies impact
Retention increased
Continuity of group process enhanced
Retreat format promotes informal exchanges

CONs Increased fatigue and vulnerability
Lack of time for integration and individual processing
Less time to build cross-cultural comfort, safety, and trust
Lack of planning time between sessions

7 Intermittent Schedule

PROs Process over time increases depth and integration
Heightens quality of group process over time
Attention to the developmental nature of training
Opportunity to experiment with new knowledge
Opportunity to alter training location
Adequate planning time between sessions

CONs Retention issues may arise

Appendix B

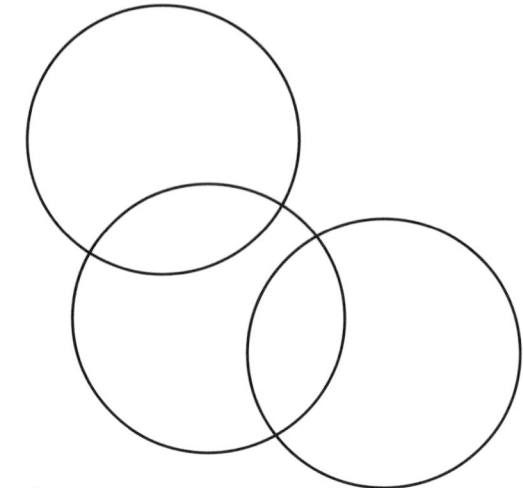

Handout: Being Direct in Supervision

What Beliefs Hold You Back From Being Direct?

1. I will hurt someone.
2. It will cause a fight. It will create conflict. There will be a power struggle.
3. I will get angry.
4. I will judge the person unjustly.
5. I will make the person feel ashamed.
6. I will be rejected.
7. I will be ostracized. I will be isolated. The student will distance himself or herself from me.
8. I will discover some attitude or feeling in myself that is unacceptable.
9. I might be wrong.
10. I might be misunderstood.
11. I might impose my own views on the student.

Protocol About Being Direct

1. Wait until an incident "arrives" in supervision related to a client or work situation.
2. Ask yourself, "What does the student's behavior tell me about the student?"
3. Voice your own feelings about bringing up your concern.

    Example 1: I feel apprehensive about bringing this up, because I know you are very hard on yourself.

    Example 2: I need us to talk about a concern I have, but I am worried that my bringing it up will cause you to pull away from me and I don't want that to happen.

4. Name your concern.

    Example 1: I am concerned about your reluctance to talk to your clients about the fact that you are Anglo and they are Mexican American.

    Example 2: I am concerned about your passivity in a situation that demands that you be assertive.

5. Ask the student how he or she is feeling about what you just brought up.

    Example 1: How are you feeling about what I just said?

    Example 2: You look angry. What do you think about the concern I raised?

6. Ask the student how he or she is feeling toward you.

    Example 1: How do you feel toward me for bringing this up?

    Example 2: You look freaked out and frozen. How are you feeling toward me for bringing it up?

    Example 3: If you didn't have to worry about my reaction, what would you really like to say to me?

7. Ask the student what he or she knows about the issue you have raised.

    Example 1: Given what I brought up, what do you know about this issue for yourself?

    Example 2: Have you had concerns yourself about this issue I just raised?

    Example 3: Has anyone else ever raised this with you before?

8. Explore the issue with the student. Do not go into an immediate solution about what he or she could do differently. (You could use any or all of the following examples.)

    Example 1: How does this play out with other clients?

    Example 2: Have bad things happened in the past when you challenged other people?

    Example 3: What do you think this is all about really?

    Example 4: What don't you understand about it? How do you feel about the issue?

    Example 5: What's the hardest thing for you about this? How do you feel about yourself right now?

9. Explore the issue relative to the impact of the issue on clients.

    Example 1: When you're passive, what do you think that's like for clients? What messages do you think you might be sending them?

Example 2: When you don't recognize the difference between you and the client, how do you think the client feels? If you were to say something, what do you think that would be like for the client?

Example 3: How do you think your client's being Korean contributes to the problem she wants help with?

10. Talk to the student about what he or she might do differently.

    Example 1: Now that we have discussed this issue some, what ideas do you have about what you might do about it? What are you worried might happen?

    Example 2: Now that we have discussed this issue some, what ideas do you have about what you might do about it? What's the worst that could happen?

11. Do something to address the student's fear.

    Example 1: Let's do some role playing for a minute. I'll be the client.

    Example 2: I understand your fear because I had that fear in bringing this issue up today. But what happened as a result of my bringing it up? We're actually closer because of it. *Or*: We're aware of a difference now that it's on the table and that's good because now we can struggle with it. Might that not be true with the client as well? After all, he or she is human just like we are.

12. Find out what happened after the interaction. (Don't let it drop.)

    Example 1: Last time we met, I brought up my concern about the racial differences between you and the clients. What happened after you left here? How did you feel? What did you think about?

    Example 2: What happened the next time you saw the client? What was different about the interaction between you? How did you feel? What do you think about all this now?

Appendix C

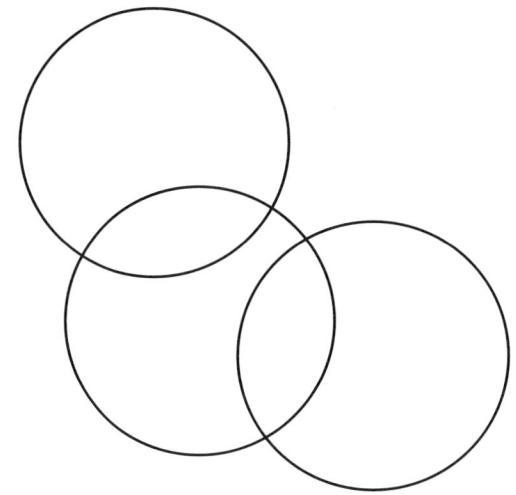

Supervision Role-Playing Examples

1. The field instructor is an immigrant from Brazil. She is in her 40s, and she is forthright and opinionated. She works at Regina Shelter, an agency for homeless adolescents and young adults. The student is an Anglo American female in her 30s who is shy and cautious. She is the first person in her working-class family to have graduated from college.

   Student: You are a student intern at Regina Shelter, an agency for homeless youth in the community. You have been working with Ket Nian, an 18-year-old Vietnamese prostitute. She recently discovered that she is pregnant. You have been trying to get her to see a doctor and are concerned about her intermittent use of drugs and how they might affect the health of the baby. However, you find that Ket Nian is passively resisting anything you suggest. You get lots of silence and "Yes, buts . . ." in response to your ideas. You are concerned because she is so young and still has the chance to better herself if she could increase her determination not to become more of a victim. You feel a little reluctant about talking to your field instructor about this because she has definite ideas about things and may be critical of the fact that you haven't been able to get Ket Nian to see a doctor yet.

   Field Instructor: This student has her placement at Regina Shelter, an agency for homeless youth in the community. You have tried to give her some young women to work with who might see her as a good role model.

2. The field instructor is a Latino male in his mid-30s who deliberates issues carefully and tries hard to be fair. He works in an agency where he is the only male. The student is an African American lesbian in her late 30s who is an advanced-standing, second-year student. She has had extensive experience working with children in schools. She is sensitive to issues of injustice and has a strong sense of right and wrong.

Student: Your second-year, advanced-standing placement is in a residential treatment facility for emotionally disturbed adolescents. Even though you have worked extensively with children in schools, you saw a young woman last week whose story hit you like a ton of bricks. The young woman was African American and talked about being tortured and sexually abused by her uncle and two brothers and threatened within an inch of her life if she told anyone. Even though she was terrified, she finally decided to tell you. You found yourself feeling so overwhelmed emotionally that you could hardly get through the session. After the session, you decided to talk to a female worker at the agency because you were worried about what was happening to you in the session. It never occurred to you to talk to your field instructor. In fact, even the thought of doing so makes you uncomfortable because you're not sure how he would react to emotions in a woman. You decide, however, that you must tell him about the client since she seems to have been pretty depressed after the session.

Field Instructor: You are a field instructor for a student who has advanced standing and extensive background working with children in schools. You both work at a residential treatment center for emotionally disturbed adolescents.

3. The field instructor is an African American female in her 40s who works at an agency for physically and developmentally disabled clients. The student, who is from Iran, is in his late 20s and has been assigned to work with male adolescents. Both field instructor and student are reserved and careful when approaching new situations.

   Student: You are an intern at Travis County Mental Health, Mental Retardation, and Physical Disability Services. You have been working with a physically disabled Caucasian male Vietnam veteran who makes jokes about foreigners and keeps asking you when you're going home. Mostly you ignore him, but during the last session he flat out asked you if anyone in your family was a suicide bomber. You know that your field instructor has a lot of experience with developmentally and physically disabled clients, but she seems sort of old school, and you're not sure where she stands with males from the Middle East. She seems to go by the book a lot, and you don't want to make her uncomfortable. However, you're at a loss how to deal with your client.

   Field Instructor: You work with developmentally disabled clients and have a student at Travis County Mental Health, Mental Retardation, and Physical Disability Services.

Appendix D

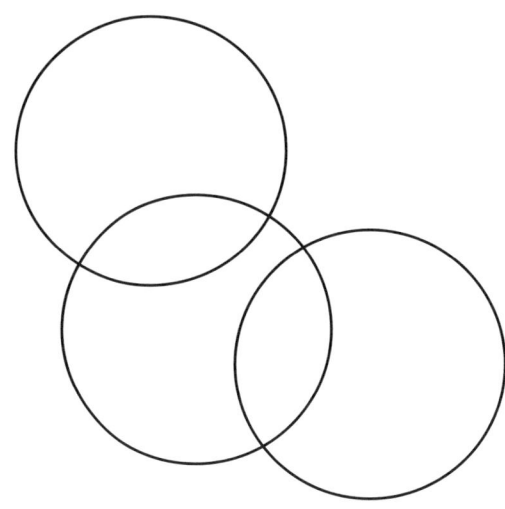

Worksheet: Assessing the Cultural Competence of the Agency

Components of Cultural Competence	Cultural Destructiveness	Cultural Blindness	Cultural Proficiency	Comments
1. Demographics of the broader community				
2. Staff's knowledge of under-represented communities				
3. Interaction with underrepresented agencies				
4. Agency practice, policy, and procedures: mission statements, bylaws, and strategic plans				
5. Agency printed materials: brochures, annual reports, outreach materials, and intake forms				
6. Agency facilities: location and accessibility				
9. Composition of staff, volunteers, and board members				
10. Role of agency as an advocate of social justice issues				
11. Organizational culture				
12. Other service delivery issues				

Overall assessment of agency's cultural competence:

Other comments and impressions:

Appendix E

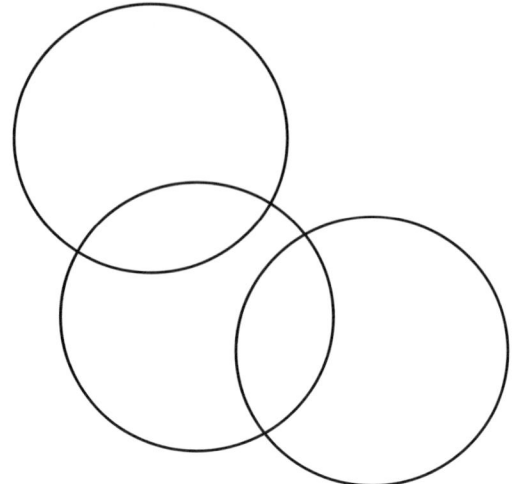

Ending and Follow-Up

_____
DATE

Agreement With Myself

1. REGARDING MYSELF, I WILL:

2. REGARDING SUPERVISION, I WILL:

3. REGARDING MY AGENCY, I WILL:

_____
DATE

Dear _____

We remember our time with you in the focus group on teaching cultural competence in field with appreciation. As promised, we are sending a copy of your "Agreement With Myself" as a gentle reminder of your commitment to doing *what you can where you are* in this important aspect of professional social work practice.

Thank you once again for your dedication to our students and to effective field teaching.

Sincerely,

_____
NAME

>Do what you can
>Where you are . . .
>You mustn't feel impotent
>Just because you are not all powerful.
>   —Lady Bird Johnson, 2001

Appendix F

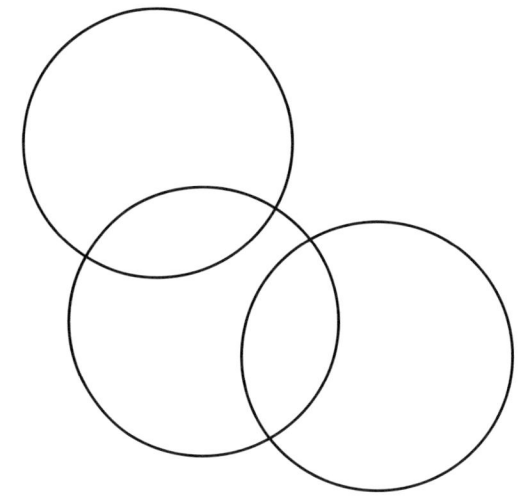

Agency Competence

CULTURAL SOPHISTICATION FRAMEWORK

	Culturally Incompetent	Culturally Sensitive
Cognitive Dimension	Oblivious	Aware
Affective Dimension	Apathetic	Sympathetic
Skills Dimension	Unskilled	Lacking some skill
Overall Effect	Destructive	Neutral

This table appears on the back page of the table of contents of: Orlandi, M. A. (1992). U.S. Department of Health and Human Services (DHHS Pub. No ADM). Washington, DC: U.S. Government Printing Office. No permission needed to reprint.

The Cultural Competence Continuum and Examples

	CULTURAL DESTRUCTIVENESS	CULTURAL INCAPACITY	CULTURAL BLINDNESS	CULTURAL PRECOMPETENCE	CULTURAL COMPETENCE	CULTURAL PROFICIENCY OR ADVANCED COMETENCE
	Most negative end of continuum	Systems do not seek to be culturally destructive, but lack capacity to help minority clients or community	Midpoint on continuum	Point on continuum that implies movement	Agencies characterized by acceptance of and respect for difference	Most positive end of continuum
Attitudes, policies, and practices that are destructive to cultures and individuals within the culture		Agency remains extremely biased; believes in racial superiority of dominant group	Agencies realize that they are unbiased because they treat everyone the same	Agency realizes its weaknesses in serving minorities and makes attempts to improve	Continuing self-assessment regarding culture	Hold culture in high esteem
Extreme examples of this orientation are programs/agencies in situations that actively participate in genocide		Paternalistic toward "lesser race"	Believe that traditional approaches that work with dominant culture are universally applicable	Agencies experiment by hiring minority staff	Continuous expansion of cultural knowledge and resources	Seek to add to knowledge base by conducting research, developing new approaches, publishing and disseminating results of demonstration projects
Examples: • Hitler's use of concentration camps • Exclusion Laws of 1885–1965 prohibited Asians from bringing spouses into country • Native American boarding schools		Channels resources away from minority groups	If it worked, all people should be able to benefit	• Explore how to reach people of color in their service area: Initiate training for their workers • Enter into needs assessments concerning minority community • Recruit minorities for boards and advisory community	Adopt service models to better meet needs of clients	Hire staff who are specialists in culturally competent practice
		Expect people of color to know their place	Make services ethnocentric; they are useless to all but the most assimilated people of color	Desire to delivery quality services	View minority groups as distinctly different from one another (have subgroups within)	Advocate for cultural competence throughout the system
		May support segregation	Ignore cultural strengths: • Encourage assimilation • Blame victims for problems	They ask, "What can we do?"	Hire unbiased employees	Walk the walk and talk the talk
		Maintain stereotypes	"Cultural deprivation model": "Something wrong with this culture"; outcomes measured by how closely client matches middle-class Anglo existence	May have a false sense of accomplishment or a failure that prevents them from moving forward	Seek advice and consultation from minority community	

CULTURAL DESTRUCTIVENESS	CULTURAL INCAPACITY	CULTURAL BLINDNESS	CULTURAL PRECOMPETENCE	CULTURAL COMPETENCE	CULTURAL PROFICIENCY OR ADVANCED COMETENCE
	Ignorance and fear of people of color	Institutional racism restricts minority access to professional training, staff positions, and services; eligibility for services often ethnocentric	"We had a Mexican American and Filipino once."	Seek minority staff who remain committed to their communities	
	Discriminatory hiring	May have special projects targeting minorities (if money is available), but little input from minority community	May believe that accomplishing one goal or activity fulfills their obligation to minority communities	Provide support to staff	
	Lower expectations of people of color	Occasionally hire minority staff, but only when it fits their needs	Tokenism—lack of information on what is possible and how to proceed		
	Subtle messages that they are not welcome or valued				
	Examples: • School segregation • Separate but equal high school counselors • Channeling people of color toward trade schools and away from colleges				

Appendix G

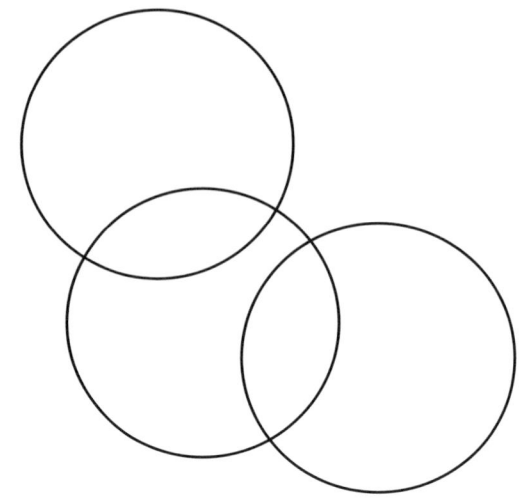

Recommended Articles

Cook, D. A. (1994). Racial identity in supervision. *Counselor Education & Supervision, 34*(2), 132–142.

    There is little empirical research on race as a variable in supervisory relationships. Cook reviews research about cross-cultural supervision from a historical perspective and draws parallels with literature on cross-cultural counseling including the use of similar research methodologies. Cook uses Helms's (1994) racial identity model to analyze the dynamics of cross-cultural supervision. She explores how racial issues might be discussed or omitted from supervision when the supervisor and supervisee exhibit various racial identity attitudes or are at different developmental stages in their racial identity. Cook argues that the unspoken assumptions regarding race and the cultural influences of the individuals involved in supervision may, indeed, affect every aspect of supervision, including the establishment of the relationship and expectations for supervision, assignment of clients, conceptualization of clients and treatment planning, recommendations for client referrals, and evaluation of supervisees. This author concludes with implications for training and for research.

Helms, J. E. (1994). Racial identity and career assessment, *Journal of Career Assessment, 2,* 199–209.

McIntosh, P. (1989). White privilege: Unpacking the invisible knapsack. In M. McGoldrick (Ed.), *Revisioning family therapy: Race, culture and gender in clinical practice* (pp. 147–152). New York: Guilford Press.

    McIntosh explains that she was taught to see racism only in individual acts of meanness, and not in invisible systems conferring dominance on her group. As a White female, this author was taught that racism was something that puts others at a disadvantage, but she has never been taught to see one of its corollary aspects, unacknowledged, White privilege. The author explains that she has come to see White privilege as an invisible package of unearned assets, like an invisible, weightless knapsack of special provisions, maps, passports, blank checks, and so on. In this article, the author lists and explains specific conditions of her daily experiences that she has taken for granted. She describes her newfound knowledge about power and privilege by stating: "Power from unearned privilege can look like strength when it is in fact permission to escape or to dominate." The author of this article articulates her thoughts, explaining that "keeping most people unaware that freedom of confident action is there for just a small number of people props up those in power and serves to keep power in the hands of the same groups that have most of it already." This article helps its readers understand that individual acts and recognition can palliate but unfortunately cannot end these privilege problems. Rather, ending the obliviousness of White privilege can help end the myth of meritocracy, the myth that democratic choice is equally available to all.

McRoy, R. G., Freeman, E. M., Logan, S. L., & Blackmon, B. (1986). Cross-cultural field supervision: Implications for social work education. *Journal of Social Work Education, 1*, 50–56.

Since the early 60s, researchers have been studying issues of race and racism in the therapeutic relationship. The major question for consideration has been whether it is possible to cross racial barriers and provide for meaningful interaction between individuals who have for so long occupied opposing positions in our society. In this classic article, McRoy et al. examined cross-cultural supervisory dyads composed of students and field instructors with particular attention to how specific racial and power dynamics affect the cross-cultural supervisory relationship. McRoy et al. found that cross-cultural field supervision, although desirable, is potentially problematic. For example, although the majority of students identified numerous problems that could occur between students and field instructors in a cross-cultural context, only a few of them cited actual problems. However, the majority of those who cited problems also expressed an extreme reluctance to discuss these with either the field instructor or the field liaison. McRoy et al. insist that supervision must acknowledge any problems that may develop and prepare students, field instructors, and field liaisons for these challenging realities. The authors conclude the article with suggestions for how to acknowledge racial conflicts as well as how to respond as an organized program in a school of social work.

Appendix H

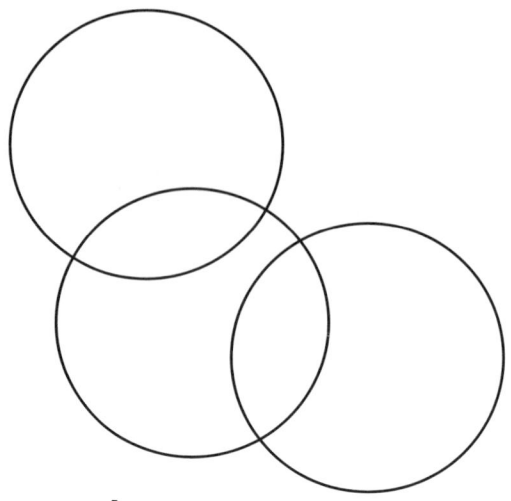

Handout: Racial Identity Development

FIGURE 5
Stages and Phases of White Racial Identity Development

PHASE 1
Abandonment of Racism

Contact → **Disintegration** → Reintegration

PHASE 2
Defining a Nonracist White Identity

Pseudo-independence → **Immersion/Emersion** → Autonomy

STAGES AND DESCRIPTION OF WHITE RACIAL IDENTITY DEVELOPMENT

Stage	Description
Contact	Oblivious to own racial identity
Disintegration	First acknowledgment of White identity
Reintegration	Idealizes Whites/denigrates Blacks
Pseudo-independence	Intellectualized acceptance of own and others' race
Immersion/Emersion	Honest appraisal of racism and significance of Whiteness
Autonomy	Internalizes a multicultural identity with nonracist Whiteness at its core

Figure 5 printed with permission from Helms, J. E. (1990). (Ed.). *Black and white racial identity: Theory, research and practice*. Westport, CT: Greenwood Press. (Figure 4.1, p. 56).

TABLE 9
Summary of General Characteristics of the Black Racial Identity Stages

IDENTITY COMPONENTS

Stages	General Themes	Emotional Themes	Reference Personal Identity	Group Orientation	Ascribed Identity
Preencounter					
Active	Idealization of Whiteness	Anxiety, poor self-esteem	Negative	White, Euro American	White
Passive	Denigration of Blackness	Defensiveness	Postive	White, Euro American	None (non-Black)
Encounter					
Events	Consciousness of race	Bitterness, hurt, anger	Postive	White Euro American	None
Experience		Euphoria	Transitional	Black	Black
Immersion/ Emersion	Idealization of Blackness	Rage, self-destructiveness	None	Black	Black
	Denigration of Whiteness	Impulsivity, euphoria	Positive	Black	Black
Internalization/ Transcendence	Racial	Self-controlled, calm, secure	Positive	Bicultural	Black
Commitment		Activistic	Positive	Pluralistic	Black/ Pan African

Table 9 printed with permission from Helms, J. E. (1990). (Ed.). *Black and white racial identity: Theory, research and practice*. Westport, CT: Greenwood Press. (Table 2.2, p. 30).

Appendix I

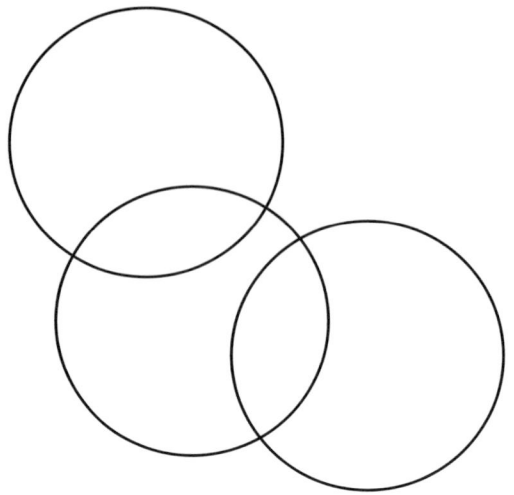

Summary of NASW Standards for Cultural Competence in Social Work Practice

Standard 1. Ethics and Values—Social workers shall function in accordance with the values, ethics, and standards of the profession, recognizing how personal and professional values may conflict with or accommodate the needs of diverse clients.

Standard 2. Self-Awareness—Social workers shall seek to develop an understanding of their own personal, cultural values and beliefs as one way of appreciating the importance of multicultural identities in the lives of people.

Standard 3. Cross-Cultural Knowledge—Social workers shall have and continue to develop specialized knowledge and understanding about the history, traditions, values, family systems, and artistic expressions of major client groups that they serve.

Standard 4. Cross-Cultural Skills—Social workers shall use appropriate methodological approaches, skills, and techniques that reflect the workers' understanding of the role of culture in the helping process.

Standard 5. Service Delivery—Social workers shall be knowledgeable about and skillful in the use of services available in the community and broader society and be able to make appropriate referrals for their diverse clients.

Standard 6. Empowerment and Advocacy—Social workers shall be aware of the effect of social policies and programs on diverse client populations, advocating for and with clients whenever appropriate.

Standard 7. Diverse Workforce—Social workers shall support and advocate for recruitment, admissions and hiring, and retention efforts in social work programs and agencies that ensure diversity within the profession.

Standard 8. Professional Education—Social workers shall advocate for and participate in educational and training programs that help advance cultural competence within the profession.

Standard 9. Language Diversity—Social workers shall seek to provide or advocate for the provision of information, referrals, and services in the language appropriate to the client, which may include use of interpreters.

Standard 10. Cross-Cultural Leadership—Social workers shall be able to communicate information about diverse client groups to other professionals.

Appendix J

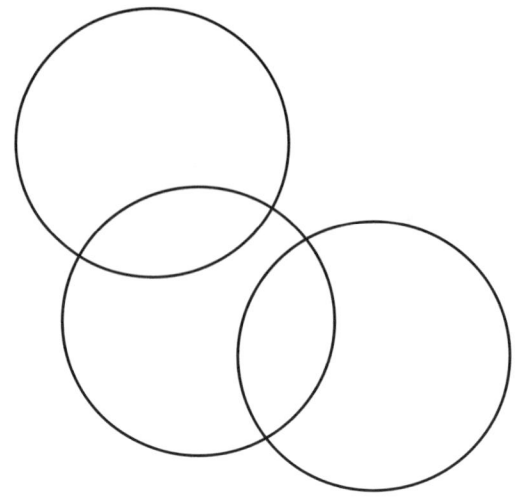

Recommended Reading

Bernard, J. M. (1994). Multicultural supervision: A reaction to Leong and Wagner, Cook, Priest, and Fukuyama. *Counselor Education and Supervision, 34,* 159–171.

Cashwell, C. S., Looby, E. J., & Housley, W. (1997). Appreciating cultural diversity through clinical supervision. *Clinical Supervisor, 15,* 75–85

Cook, D. (1994). Racial identity in supervision. *Counselor education and supervision, 34,* 132–141.

Cook, D. A. (1983). *A survey of ethnic minority clinical and counseling graduate student's perceptions of their cross cultural supervision experiences.* Unpublished doctoral dissertation, Southern Illinois University, Carbondale.

Cook, D. A., & Helms, J. E. (1988). Visible racial/ethnic group supervisees' satisfaction with cross-cultural supervision as predicted by relationship characteristics. *Journal of Counseling Psychology, 35*(3), 268–274.

Davenport, D. S., & Yurich, J. M. (1991). Multicultural gender issues. *Journal of Counseling and Development, 70,* 64–71.

Fukuyama, M. A. (1994). Critical incidents in multicultural counseling supervision: A phenomenological approach to supervision research. *Counselor Education and Supervision, 34,* 142–151.

Gant, L. M., Nadda, B. A., Brabson, H. V., Jayaratne, S., Chess, W. A., & Singh, A. (1993). Effects of social support and undermining on African-American workers' perceptions of co-worker and supervisor relationships and psychological well-being. *Social Work, 38,* 158–164.

Helms, J. (1990). *Black and white racial identity: Theory, research and practice.* Westport, CT: Praeger.

Hendricks, C. O. (2003) Learning and teaching cultural competence in the practice of social work *Journal of Teaching in Social Work, 23,* 73–86.

Hilton, D. B., Russell, R. K., & Salmi, S. W. (1995). The effects of supervisor's race and level of support on perceptions of supervision. *Journal of Counseling and Development, 73*, 559–563.

Jayaratne, S., Brabson, H. V., Gant, L. M., Nadda, B. A., Singh, A., & Chess, W. A. (1992). African-American practitioners' perceptions of their supervisors: Emotional support, social undermining, and criticism. *Administration in Social Work, 16*(2), 27–43.

Johnson, A. G. (2001). *Privilege, power, and difference.* Boston: McGraw-Hill.

Manoleas, P. (2004). The field practicum as the focus point for training diversity-competent MSW social workers. In L. Gutiérrez, M. E. Zuñiga, & D. Lum (Eds.), *Education for multicultural social work practice: Critical viewpoints and future directions* (pp. 237–250). Alexandria, VA: Council on Social Work Education.

Marshack, E. F., Hendricks, C. O., & Gladstein, M. (1994). The commonality of difference: Teaching about diversity in field instruction. *Journal of Multicultural Social Work, 3*(1), 77–89.

McIntosh, P. (1989, July/August). White privilege: Unpacking the invisible knapsack. In M. McGoldrick (Ed.), *Revisioning family therapy: Race, culture and gender in clinical practice* (pp. 147–152). New York: Guilford Press.

McRoy, R. G., Freeman, E. M., Logan, S. L., & Blackmon, B. (1986). Cross-cultural field supervision: Implications for social work education. *Journal of Social Work Education, 22*(1), 50–55.

Miller, J., Hyde, C., & Ruth, B. J. (2004). Teaching about race and racism in social work: The challenge for white educators. *Smith College Studies in Social Work, 74*, 409–426.

Mishna, F., & Rasmussen, B. (2001). The learning relationship: Working through disjunctions in the classroom. *Clinical Social Work Journal, 29*, 387–399.

Priddy, W. W. (2004). Multicultural competence in the field practicum. In L. Gutiérrez, M. E. Zuñiga, & D. Lum (Eds.), *Education for multicultural social work practice: Critical viewpoints and future directions* (pp. 237–250). Alexandria, VA: Council on Social Work Education.

Reynolds, A. L., & Pope, R. L. (1991). The complexities of diversity: Exploring multiple oppressions. *Journal of Counseling and Development 70*, 174–180.

Skillings, J., & Dobbins, J. (1991). Racism as a disease: Etiology and treatment implications. *Journal of Counseling and Development, 70*, 206–212.

Solomon, B. (1982). Power: The troublesome factor in cross-cultural supervision. *Smith College School of Social Work Journal, 10*(1), 27–32.

Van Soest, D. (2004). Structural barriers to multicultural competence in the field practicum. In L. Gutiérrez, M. Zuñiga, & D. Lum (Eds.), *Education for multicultural social work practice* (pp. 265–278), Alexandria, VA: Council on Social Work Education.